The Book of Isaiah

The Book of Isaiah

An Exposition by
Charles R. Erdman

BAKER BOOK HOUSE
Grand Rapids, Michigan 49506

50.09

OCLC #
09265508

PHOTOLITHOPRINTED BY CUSHING - MALLOY, INC.
ANN ARBOR, MICHIGAN, UNITED STATES OF AMERICA

Contents

His Name Shall Be Called
Wonderful Counselor, The Mighty God,
The Everlasting Father, The Prince of Peace

Introduction

ISAIAH was a princely character, a wise and patriotic statesman, a gifted poet, and a divinely inspired prophet. He may not have been of noble birth, as some have supposed; but his heroic courage, his spotless purity, his sympathy with the poor, his hatred of sham and pretense, his exalted ideals and his unfailing faith in God gave him a more royal rank than any kingly pedigree could have conferred. His messages concerned Judah and Jerusalem. While his vision was world-wide, he was concerned with other nations only as they were related to his people.

His call to prophetic service came in the last year of King Uzziah (740 B.C.). The long and brilliant reign of this monarch had brought Judah to a peak of prosperity and power which had not been known since the days when the ten Northern Tribes had revolted to form the kingdom of Israel. However, prosperity had encouraged pride and corruption, luxury and cruelty and a fatal forgetfulness of God. In his later years the king was smitten with leprosy, and his pitiful plight has been regarded as a parable of the moral condition of his people. He was succeeded by Jotham, a king of good intention, but lacking the strength to turn the currents of the national life. His son Ahaz proved to be possibly the worst ruler that had occupied the throne of Judah. His rule was attended by moral corruption and political disaster. It was early in his reign that Isaiah made his first recorded appearance as a counselor in affairs of state. The two small kingdoms of Israel and Syria had united in an endeavor to stem the advance of the mighty empire of Assyria. Probably in order to compel Ahaz to join their confederacy, they invaded the territory of Judah. King and people were terrified.

Then Isaiah came forward with his inspired message. He declared that there was no need of fear; within two or three years the lands of the enemies would be laid waste; but he added a prophecy of punishment for Judah, unless the nation should repent and put its trust in God.

This counsel offered by Isaiah proved to be fruitless. Ahaz appealed to Assyria for aid. This was promptly given, but at the price of freedom. Judah was made a vassal state. The kingdom of Israel was destroyed and thousands of the people were carried away captive (722 B.C.).

The next year Hezekiah succeeded Ahaz as king of Judah. He restored the temple worship, opposed idolatry, and did much toward recovering the power of Judah. However, the political horizon was dark. The cruel hosts of Assyria were threatening and irresistible. Again and again the land was invaded and the life of the nation imperiled. The king was advised by his nobles to form alliances with Egypt and with the smaller neighboring nations. Against such perilous coalitions Isaiah protested. He advised strict neutrality, and a patient waiting for divine deliverance. He voiced his warnings in a variety of ways, by eloquent orations, by personal audiences with the king, by giving to his two sons symbolic and prophetic names, by publicly posting a great placard on which one of these names was printed, even by appearing in the streets of Jerusalem barefoot and clothed in the wretched garments of a captive as a warning to those who would not trust or obey the Lord.

In his early years King Hezekiah was smitten by a disease which Isaiah predicted would be fatal. In response to his own agonizing prayer, the king was healed, and Isaiah predicted that fourteen years would be added to his life. About that time an embassy arrived from the king of Babylon, ostensibly to congratulate King Hezekiah on his recovery, but probably to urge him to unite in an endeavor to throw off the yoke of Assyria. Hezekiah, in foolish pride, displayed to the Babylonian envoys the treasures of his palace and his arsenal, as though these and not the living God were the source of his strength and the grounds of his hope. Against this folly Isaiah spoke in stern rebuke and delivered what was possibly his most astounding prophecy. He predicted that all Hezekiah's riches would be carried to Babylon, and yet this prediction was made at the time when Assyria was the world power and Babylon was still in the position of an inferior vassal. This was the first clear vision of the Babylonian captivity, with which the later chapters of the Book of Isaiah were concerned, and beyond which captivity the prophet caught bright vistas of redemption and return.

In reality Assyria was now at the height of its heartless power, and the attempt on the part of the smaller nations to throw off the yoke of submission was visited with bitter penalties. When Hezekiah was persuaded by his counselors to refuse further tribute (701 B.C.), Judah was invaded and Jerusalem, for a time, was spared only when the king had paid a ransom so exorbitant as to rob the treasure-house and to strip the Temple of its gold. Even this did not satisfy the Assyrian invader. He broke his pledge and demanded the surrender of the city. This was the supreme hour in the life of Isaiah. His solemn warnings and severe rebukes now gave place to messages of hope and cheer. He stood alone among the terrified and helpless counselors of the king. With exultant assurance he declared that the sacred city would not fall into the hands of the haughty and insolent conqueror. A miracle occurred. The God who had spoken through Isaiah stretched out His hand. In a single night 185,000 of the enemy were destroyed, and the shattered hosts were withdrawn to Assyria, not to return during the lifetime of the prophet. Isaiah's faith had been vindicated, and during the few remaining years of the reign of Hezekiah the position of the prophet was one of security and honor, yet his fondest dreams were not realized. He had expected that the goodness of God would bring the people to a position of grateful obedience and trust; but when Manasseh succeeded his father on the throne, all the national policies were reversed. Foreign alliances were made and idolatry restored. Those who were followers of Isaiah were persecuted, and, according to tradition, the prophet himself suffered a cruel death as a martyr. However, he left a priceless heritage in the messages which he had given to his own time and nation and to the people of God of all the ages to come.

These messages, as they have been preserved, are largely in the form of poems. They can be appreciated best when so printed, as in most recent editions of the Bible. They constitute the very climax and glory of Hebrew literature. The majesty and beauty of their diction, their brilliant word pictures, their breadth of vision, their challenging rebukes, their tender appeals, their amazing variety of style, now sounding a voice of thunder and now full of silent tears, these characterize a body of poetic compositions which never has been surpassed.

The poems which constitute the Book of Isaiah are divided into two parts by a section of history (Chs. 36 to 39). This section records the threat and retreat of the Assyrians under the leadership of Sennacherib, the sickness and recovery of Hezekiah, and the visit of an embassy from Babylon.

The first portion of the Book (Chs. 1 to 35) consists chiefly of charges against Judah and in predictions of punishment. These are interspersed, however, with gleams of the glory which will follow repentance and pardon. The great enemy here depicted is Assyria, the world power.

The second portion of the Book (Chs. 40 to 60) presents prophecies of deliverance and restoration. Here the enemy is the mighty empire of Babylon, by whose rulers Judah has been carried captive.

In the first portion, after a general introduction (Ch. 1), Judah is charged with ingratitude and apostasy; punishment is predicted, but also pardon and future glory (Chs. 2–5). Isaiah is called to a prophetic ministry which will result in hardening the hearts of the people, but in the salvation of a remnant through whom the future glory can be attained (Ch. 6).

The Book of Immanuel (Chs. 7 to 12) predicts divine protection from the armies of Syria and Israel (Ephraim), and a more notable deliverance from the hosts of Assyria. This is to be effected by a king, "from the stem of Jesse," who will establish peace and whose righteous reign will call forth a thankful hymn of praise.

There follow two Books of Burdens (Chs. 13 to 23), or prophecies of judgment upon the nations whose fortunes were related to Judah and Jerusalem. These ten Burdens are divided into two series, of five each, by a brief paragraph (Ch. 20). This describes the symbolic action of Isaiah, when for three years he appeared in the garb of a captive, to picture the fate of Egypt and of all who trusted in Egypt for help.

Once again, in this series of warnings, Isaiah pauses. Just before the Ninth Burden, he denounces Shebna, the court treasurer, for a foreign policy opposed to that of Isaiah and the king (Ch. 22:14–25).

As a grand finale to these Books of Burdens there is recorded a prophecy of the "Day of the Lord." This is a sublime prediction of universal divine judgment, and is contrasted with the redemption and joy of the restored people of God (Chs. 24 to 27).

The cycle of prophecies which closes the first great section of Isaiah, constitutes what has been known as the *Book of Woes*. These prophecies are mainly warnings against the false hopes of dependence

on Egypt and predictions of punishment on the enemies of Judah. They contain fierce denunciation of
Assyria and Edom, but also picture such deliverance
and glory for Judah as transcend all human experience (Chs. 28 to 35).

The events which are recorded in the *Historical
Section* of Isaiah (Chs. 36 to 39) do not appear in the
order of time, but are arranged according to literary
art. The illness and recovery of Hezekiah and the visit
of the embassy from Babylon preceded the invasion
and the retreat of the Assyrians, but the latter are
mentioned first because in all the earlier chapters
Assyria has been the world power and the threat of
Assyria has been always the dark cloud on the horizon;
but, in the remaining chapters of the Book, Babylon
will be the world power and the prophecies will relate
to the Babylonian captivity of Judah. Therefore this
Historical Section, thus arranged, becomes a proper
appendix to Chapters 1 to 35 and an introduction to
Chapters 40 to 66.

These last chapters form the matchless *Prophecies of Restoration.* They may be divided into three
sections of nine chapters each. The first section glori-
fies the *power of God,* by whom deliverance is to be
accomplished. His agent is to be Cyrus, the king of
Persia, whose decree in 536 B.C. permitted the return
of the Jews and the rebuilding of Jerusalem and its
Temple (Chs. 40 to 48).

The second section predicts a more marvelous redemption, namely, a moral and spiritual deliverance
from apostasy and iniquity and sin. The agent by
whom this is to be made possible is designated *"the*

Servant of the Lord" (Jehovah). This term applied first of all to the nation, then more specifically to a believing and chosen "remnant" of the people, and finally to a divine Person, the Saviour and Redeemer. Deliverance was to be achieved by innocent and vicarious suffering. Such a prophecy is treasured as a specific prediction of the saving work of Christ (Chs. 49 to 57).

These majestic "prophecies of restoration" reach their climax in the third section, which depicts the glorious future of Judah and the splendors of the *perfected kingdom of God.* The fulfillment was found in the return of the captives from Babylon, but more notably in the earthly ministry of our Saviour (Luke 4:17–21). Yet, the radiant horizon widens until the prophet beholds all nations rejoicing in the rule of the Servant of the Lord who has become the King of kings, and the everlasting Prince of Peace.

C.R.E.

The Book of Isaiah

I

PROPHECIES OF PUNISHMENT

Isaiah 1 to 35

1. THE GUILT OF JUDAH [CHS. 1 TO 5]

THE ANCIENT Hebrew prophets spoke for their own age and to their own people. Yet their words embodied abiding principles and their predictions extended into the distant future. Their messages are pertinent to the modern world and are particularly precious to those readers who have found that "the testimony of Jesus is the spirit of prophecy."

The hearers to whom Isaiah spoke, and the period in which he lived, are defined in the first verse of his prophecies:

"The vision of Isaiah the Son of Amoz, which he saw concerning Judah and Jerusalem in the days of Uzziah, Jotham, Ahaz, and Hezekiah, kings of Judah."

Thus the prophet is not so much concerned with the Northern Kingdom of Israel, or with the other nations which he names, but chiefly with Judah and its capital, the sacred city of Jerusalem.

He calls his message a "vision." He "sees"; he penetrates beneath the surface of events and sets forth the changeless laws of God; he looks beyond the present and beholds a still distant future. His diverse prophecies form a unit. They are one "vision." The substance is always the same. It is summarized in apostasy, punishment, repentance, restoration.

Thus the *first chapter* forms an introduction to the entire Book. It strikes all those chief notes which again will be sounded. "Apostasy" is here presented, first of all, as senseless, stupid, ingratitude, and rebellion. To this divine indictment the prophet summons the whole universe as witness:

> Hear, O heavens, and give ear, O earth
>   for the Lord has spoken:
> I have nourished and brought up children,
>   and they have rebelled against me.
> The ox knoweth his owner,
>   and the ass his master's crib;
> but Israel doth not know,
>   my people doth not consider.
> Ah sinful nation,
>   a people laden with iniquity,
> a seed of evildoers,
>   children that are corrupters:
> They have forsaken the Lord,
>   they have provoked the Holy One of Israel
>   unto anger,
> they are gone away backward.

This senseless apostasy has resulted in a moral and spiritual state which Isaiah depicts under the figure of a loathsome disease:

> Why should ye be stricken any more?
>   ye will revolt more and more:

The whole head is sick,
  and the whole heart faint.
From the sole of the foot even unto the head
  there is no soundness in it;
but wounds and bruises,
  and putrifying sores;
they have not been closed, neither bound up,
  neither mollified with ointment.

The moral condition has been accompanied by political disaster. Judah has been invaded and laid waste. Jerusalem has been surrounded by the enemy. Had it not been for divine intervention the nation would have been completely destroyed:

Your country is desolate,
  your cities are burned with fire:
your land, strangers devour it
  in your presence, and it is desolate,
as overthrown by strangers.
And the daughter of Zion is left
  as a cottage in a vineyard,
as a lodge in a garden of cucumbers,
  as a besieged city.
Except the Lord of hosts
  had left unto us a very small remnant,
we should have been as Sodom,
  and we should have been like unto Gomorrah.

It is easy to imagine what the people might have answered to such an indictment: "Why do you call us apostate? We are the most religious people in the world. Just see our crowded Temple, our countless feasts."

Isaiah replies: *Ceremonial* cannot save. Indeed, religious forms aside from faith and righteousness meet with only divine displeasure.

> Hear the word of the Lord,
>   ye rulers of Sodom:
> give ear unto the law of our God,
>   ye people of Gomorrah.
> To what purpose is the multitude
>   of your sacrifices unto me?
>   saith the Lord:
> I am full of the burnt offerings of rams,
>   and the fat of fed beasts:
> and I delight not in the blood of bullocks,
>   or of lambs, or of he goats (vs. 1–11).

This was not to repudiate the sacrificial system or the laws of Moses, but to rebuke an attempt to substitute ritual forms for penitence and obedience.

To worship in the Temple only as a ceremony is but to "trample" the sacred courts. Incense and holy days are merely a weariness to the Lord. Prayers offered with outstretched hands stained with blood are an insult to God (vs. 12–15).

There is one condition of acceptable worship. This condition is sincere repentance manifest in deeds of purity and charity. This is certain to receive divine pardon and cleansing, and will result in a restoration of national life:

> *Come now, and let us reason together,*
>   *saith the Lord:*

though your sins be as scarlet,
  they shall be as white as snow;
though they be red like crimson,
  they shall be as wool.

Neither the fact that it was addressed to Judah first nor the changes of intervening centuries has dimmed the music or diminished the power of this divine appeal. It has inspired hope in the hearts of countless despairing souls. In all ages it has brought relief to those who were tortured by the consciousness of guilt, and has led them to find new life and peace in the power of redeeming love (vs. 16–20).

But would the people of Judah repent and "eat the good of the land," or "refuse and rebel" and "be devoured by the sword"? Isaiah expects and predicts the best; but this can come only through purifying judgments. The present is dark enough.

How is the faithful city
    become an harlot!
it was full of judgment;
    righteousness lodged in it;
  but now murderers.
Thy silver is become dross,
  thy wine mixed with water:
Thy princes are rebellious,
  and companions of thieves:
every one loveth gifts,
  and followeth after rewards:
they judge not the fatherless,
    neither doth the cause of the
    widow come unto them.

Yet, with unconquerable faith, the prophet beholds a brighter future in which iniquity has been purged away:

> And I will turn my hand upon thee,
>   and purely purge away thy dross,
>   and take away all thy tin:
> And I will restore thy judges as at the first,
>   and thy counsellors as at the beginning:
> afterward thou shalt be called, The city of right-
>   eousness,
>   the faithful city.
> Zion shall be redeemed with judgment,
>   and her converts with righteousness (vs. 21–27).

The change will be effected by experiences of humiliation and shame. The people would be "like an oak whose leaf has withered, and like a garden without water"; the impenitent would perish with their works; yet out of the purifying fires finally would arise "the city of righteousness" (Ch. 1:28–29).

Following the pattern set in the introductory chapter, the next discourses continue the indictment of Judah and predict the judgments which will be necessary to secure repentance and restoration. *Chapters 2 and 4* form a cycle which begins and ends with a prophecy of future glory, but which includes pictures of present apostasy and impending doom.

The vision of Zion redeemed and exalted is one of unsurpassed beauty and dignity. It indicates what this world might be if God were accepted as its Ruler and men were governed by His laws.

And it shall come to pass in the last days,
    that the mountain of the Lord's house
shall be established in the top of the mountains,
    and shall be exalted above the hills;
and all nations shall flow unto it.
And many people shall go and say,
    Come ye, and let us go up to the mountain of
      the Lord,
to the house of the God of Jacob;
    and he will teach us his ways,
and we will walk in his paths:
    For out of Zion shall go forth the law,
and the word of the Lord from Jerusalem.
    And he shall judge among the nations,
and shall rebuke many people:
    and they shall beat their swords into plow-
      shares,
and their spears into pruninghooks:
    nation shall not lift up sword against nation,
neither shall they learn war any more (Ch. 2:1–4).

With such a vision before him, the prophet makes his pathetic appeal:

O house of Jacob, come, let us walk
    in the light of the Lord (v. 5).

There is no answer. With the ideal of a glorious future for Jerusalem as the seat of worship which will attract all nations the present state of the city is in dark contrast.

Instead of serving God, the people are seeking for sorcerers and magicians. They are trusting in their material prosperity and in their implements of war.

They are given wholly to idolatry. They are under
the divine displeasure.

> Therefore thou hast forsaken thy people
>   the house of Jacob,
> because they be replenished from the east,
>   and are soothsayers like the Philistines,
> and they please themselves in the children of
>   strangers.
> Their land also is full of silver and gold,
>   neither is there any end of their treasures;
> their land is also full of horses,
>   neither is there any end of their chariots:
> Their land also is full of idols;
>   they worship the work of their own hands,
> that which their own fingers have made.

Therefore the Lord must visit His people with
punishment to humble their pride and to bring them
to repentance and to trust in Him:

> For the day of the Lord of hosts
>   shall be upon every one that is proud and lofty,
> and upon every one that is lifted up;
>   and he shall be brought low. . . .
> In that day a man shall cast his idols of silver,
>   and his idols of gold,
> which they made each one for himself to worship,
>   to the moles and to the bats.
> To go into the clefts of the rocks,
>   and into the tops of the ragged rocks,
> for fear of the Lord, and for the glory of his
>   majesty,

when he ariseth to shake terribly the earth
(vs. 6–22).

The present godlessness of the people is resulting in social and political confusion and chaos. Inso-
lence and impotence, poverty and injustice abound.
No one is willing to accept public office. Any man
who is decently clad is regarded as thereby qualified
for a government position. Those who do possess
power are accused of cruelty and greed:

The Lord will enter into judgment with the ancients
of his people, and the princes thereof: for ye have eaten
up the vineyard; the spoil of the poor is in your houses.
What mean ye that ye beat my people to pieces, and grind
the faces of the poor? saith the Lord God of hosts (Ch. 3:
1–15).

The crowning, if not the chief, indictment is addressed to the women of Judah. They are pictured as
proud, selfish, extravagant, senseless. In a time of
national crisis and of social distress their whole
thoughts are centered on their perfumes, their jew-
elry, their cosmetics, their clothing. The prophet
mentions twenty-one articles of dress commonly
worn. In penning this paragraph it well may be
supposed he had the help of that "prophetess," his
wife. He was not presuming to dictate the proper apparel for women, only to indicate that vain, indul-
gent, careless womanhood surely indicates the decay
of national life. In contrast to the luxury and display
of the present days, the prophet predicts the coming
judgment, when their ornaments and finery would
be exchanged for the rags and the repulsiveness of

slaves. The fall of their city was at hand. So few men
would be left that these women, no longer courted
and wooed, would strive in eager rivalry for the benefits which marriage might afford.

> Thy men shall fall by the sword,
>   and thy mighty in the war. . . .
> And in that day seven women shall take hold of
>   one man, saying,
> We will eat our own bread, and wear our own ap-
>   parel: only
> let us be·called by thy name, to take away our re-
>   proach (vs. 3–16 to 4:1).

In contrast with this dark picture the *fourth
chapter* is bright with the promise of deliverance and
restoration. Thus the discourse, which began with the
superb vision of Zion exalted among the nations (Ch.
2:2–4), now comes to the close with the description
of a people purified and pardoned, and so prepared for
their high destiny as a source of blessing to all the
world. The land once desolated is now beautiful with
verdure and fruitfulness. The city which had been
stained by guilt is now cleansed and purged, and the
transformed remnant of its inhabitants dedicated to
the service of God and so worthy to be enrolled as citizens of Zion. The chief feature of all is the glorious
presence of the Lord. This is painted with colors borrowed from the wilderness experience of ancient Israel when the divine presence was manifested by the
pillar of cloud and of fire.

The Lord will create over the whole site of Mount
Zion and over her assemblies a cloud by day, and smoke

and the shining of a flaming fire by night; for over all the glory there will be a canopy and a pavilion. It will be for a shade by day from the heat, and for a refuge and a shelter from the storm and rain (Ch. 4:2–6).

Thus the presence of God is now the shield and protection of His people during their earthly journey; it will be the glory and light of the Heavenly City.

In his *fifth chapter* the prophet continues to denounce the guilt of Judah. He has recourse to parable and song. To show the sinful ingratitude of the people he sings the *Song of the Vineyard* (vs. 1–7). He then pronounces a series of six *woes* against specific sins (vs. 8–23), and concludes by a terrifying announcement of the near approach of *judgment* (vs. 24–30).

The *vineyard* belonged to his beloved friend. Upon it had been bestowed the most generous care, but it had brought forth only wild grapes.

> Now will I sing to my well-beloved
>   a song of my beloved touching his vineyard.
> My well-beloved hath a vineyard
>   in a very fruitful hill:
> And he fenced it, and gathered out the stones
>   thereof,
>   and planted it with the choicest vines,
> and built a tower in the midst of it,
>   and also made a winepress therein:
> and he looked that it should bring forth grapes,
>   and it brought forth wild grapes.

The singer then appeals to his hearers to judge between his friend and his vineyard. Was there anything more that the owner could have done?

> And now, O inhabitants of Jerusalem,
>> and men of Judah,
> judge, I pray you,
>> betwixt me and my vineyard.

The meaning of the parable already must be plain, but the Song ends in a clear interpretation which conveys a severe rebuke:

> For the vineyard of the Lord of hosts
>> is the house of Israel,
> and the men of Judah are his pleasant planting;
>> and he looked for justice,
> but behold oppression,
>> for righteousness
> but behold a cry (Ch. 5:1–7).

The Song began with a note of true tenderness; it is followed by bitter predictions. Woes are pronounced against (1) insatiable greed:

> Woe unto them that join house to house,
>> that lay field to field,
> till there be no place,
>> that they may be placed alone
> in the midst of the earth!
> In my hearing the Lord of hosts hath sworn:
>> Of a truth many houses shall be desolate,
> even great and fair, without inhabitant.
> Yea, ten acres of vineyard shall yield one bath,
>> and the seed of an homer shall yield an ephah
>>> (vs. 8–10).

(2) Unbridled and godless dissipation, as pictured in verses 11 and 12, can result only in captivity, in death, and desolation.

> Woe unto them that rise up early in the morning,
>   that they may follow strong drink;
> that continue until night,
>   till wine inflame them!
> And the harp, and the viol,
> the tabret, and pipe, and wine,
>   are in their feasts:
> but they regard not the work of the Lord,
>   neither consider the operation of his hands
>   (vs. 11–12).

Such sensual indulgence and selfish glory "lead but to the grave":

> Therefore hell hath enlarged herself,
>   and opened her mouth without measure:
> and their glory and their multitude,
>   and their pomp, and he that rejoiceth,
> shall descend into it.

So great will be the desolation that sheep will find pasture and nomad tribes will wander freely among the ruins of the city and in the desolated gardens (vs. 13–17).

(3) Woe is pronounced upon those who are bound as the servants of sin, and are certain to suffer punishment, yet defy the Almighty and challenge Him to hasten His judgments so that they can see them.

> Woe unto them that draw iniquity with cords of
>   vanity,
>   and sin as it were with a cart rope:
> That say, Let him make speed,
>   and hasten his work, that we may see it:
> and let the counsel of the Holy One of Israel draw
>   nigh and come,
>   that we may know it! (vs. 18–19).

So, too, woe is predicted (4) for those whose moral judgments have become so confused that they "call evil good, and good evil: that put darkness for light, and light for darkness; that put bitter for sweet, and sweet for bitter!" (v. 20).

(5) The fifth woe is directed against such conceited and ignorant sensualists as were continually opposing Isaiah and counseling the king to form senseless foreign alliances and to undertake hopeless wars.

> Woe unto them that are wise in their own eyes,
>   and prudent in their own sight! (v. 21).

The intemperance which is the underlying cause of most of the evils upon which woes have been pronounced is the evident source of the corruption which is denounced in the concluding warning. Even the judges were victims of drink and were condemned as those

> Which justify the wicked for reward,
>   and deprive the innocent of his right (vs.
>   22–23).

On a nation guilty of such iniquities punishment is certain to fall. Its near approach is painted under the picture of an invading army. The Assyrian hosts are hastening in answer to the call of God who summons them as the instrument of His purifying judgment. Such an army never wearies nor sleeps. Its speed is like the wind. Its attack is fierce as that of a young lion.

> And he will lift up an ensign to the nations from
> > far,
> > and will hiss unto them from the end of the
> > > earth:
> and behold they shall come with speed swiftly:
> > none shall be weary nor stumble among them;
> none shall slumber nor sleep;
> > neither shall the girdle of their loins be loosed,
> nor the latchet of their shoes be broken:
> > whose arrows are sharp,
> and all their bows bent,
> > their horses' hoofs shall be counted like flint,
> and their wheels like a whirlwind:
> > their roaring shall be like a lion,
> they shall roar like young lions:
> > yea, they shall roar, and lay hold of the prey,
> and shall carry it away safe,
> > and none shall deliver it.
> And in that day they shall roar against them
> > like the roaring of the sea:
> and if one look unto the land,
> > behold darkness and sorrow,
> and the light is darkened in the heavens thereof
> > (vs. 24–30).

With such an indictment of guilt, and such predictions of punishment, there was need of a prophet who would interpret the dealings of God and, beyond the dark horizon of doom, would see for Judah bright vistas of hope and glory. Such a prophet was Isaiah, the most majestic and eloquent of the ancient messengers of God.

2. THE CALL OF THE PROPHET [CH. 6]

Isaiah must have been called to his prophetic ministry long before he composed the paragraphs which comprise the opening chapters of the Book. He was summoned to address a people such as those chapters describe. The nation was too hardened in heart by far to heed his words of warning, too much in need of purifying judgments to escape the predicted punishments, yet so precious in the sight of God that it was yet to fulfil a glorious mission to the world. These are the three features in this record of Isaiah's "call"— first, the unwillingness of the nation to accept his message; second, the desolation of the land and the captivity of the people, and, third, the salvation of a purified remnant through which the gracious purpose of God would be fulfilled.

The time of the "call" is specified as "the year in which king Uzziah died." This is not only a date but also a description. It marks a time of crisis in the history of the nation. The brilliant reign of the king had ended in tragedy and terror. The monarch had been smitten by a loathsome disease, and when he died the people already had been threatened by two perils. The first was the moral decay which prosperity and luxury had engendered; the second was the political danger which the rising power of Assyria embodied.

It seems that on a certain day Isaiah was worshiping in the temple and probably was pondering the future of his people, when suddenly the walls of the temple dissolved and disappeared, and he was standing in the court of heaven. Thus the prophet records his own experience:

I saw also the Lord sitting upon a throne, high and lifted up, and his train filled the temple. Above it stood the seraphim: each one had six wings; with twain he covered his face, and with twain he covered his feet, and with twain he did fly. And one cried unto another, and said,

Holy, holy, holy, is the Lord of hosts:
The whole earth is full of his glory.

And the foundations of the thresholds shook at the voice of him that cried, and the house was filled with smoke (vs. 1–4).

The essence of *the vision* was an expression of the holiness of God, that is, of his infinite purity, and majesty and power, of his "separation" from all limits of goodness, of justice, of grace. Yet, who was this Being? Was He merely created by the fancy of a prophet? Has His "holiness" never been revealed? Isaiah answers: "The whole earth is filled with his glory," with his "manifested excellence." The Apostle John, with splendid audacity, implies that this vision finds its complete expression in our Lord Jesus Christ:

These things said Isaiah because he saw his glory; and he spake of him (John 12:41).

The effect of the vision is the *contrition* of the prophet, his confession of sin, and his utter unworthiness to live in the presence of such holiness:

> Then said I,
> "Woe is me! for I am undone;
> Because I am a man of unclean lips,
> And I dwell in the midst of a people of unclean
>   lips,
> For mine eyes have seen the King,
> The LORD of hosts!"

Such contrition is immediately followed by *cleansing*:

> Then flew one of the seraphim unto me, having a live coal in his hand, which he had taken with the tongs from off the altar: and he laid it upon my mouth, and said, Lo, this hath touched thy lips; and thine iniquity is taken away, and thy sin purged.

One who has the sense of divine pardon usually hears a call to service, and responds in a spirit of grateful, sincere *consecration*:

> Also I heard the voice of the Lord, saying, Whom shall I send, and who will go for us? Then said I, Here am I; send me.

The *commission* given to Isaiah was difficult in the extreme and was a challenge to his courage. He was to rebuke the nation for its moral blindness and its stubborn impenitence. This was to be his message:

> Hear ye indeed, but understand not
> and see ye indeed, but perceive not.

The very effect of his pleading was to make the people more callous and less able to repent. This was not to be the purpose of his prophecies, but would be the result:

> Make the heart of this people fat,
> And their ears heavy,
> And shut their eyes,
> Lest they see with their eyes
> And hear with their ears,
> And understand with their hearts,
> And turn and be healed.

No wonder that Isaiah cries in dismay, "Lord, how long?" Was there to be none to heed? Was there to be no end to the rebellion of his people? The divine reply was that penitence could come only by the fiery process of punishment, of decimation, of desolation, of captivity. Even a fraction which might escape would need to be purged and purified.

> Thus to the question, "How long?" came the divine reply:
> "Until cities lie waste without inhabitant,
> and houses without men,
> and the land is utterly desolate,
> and the Lord removes men far away,
> and the forsaken places are many
> in the midst of the land.
> And though a tenth remain in it,
> it shall in turn be burned:
> as a terebinth or an oak,
> whose stock remains standing when it is felled;
> so the holy seed is its stock."

The work of Isaiah, however, was not to be a failure. He was not being called to mere disappointment and defeat. There would be, as a result of his pleadings and his prophecies, a repentant remnant, the beginning of a new people, by which the life of the nation would be preserved and from which would come the Saviour of the world.

3. THE BOOK OF IMMANUEL [CHS. 7–12]

Isaiah continues his arraignment of Judah. In the earlier addresses (chs. 1–6) he has condemned the people because of social and personal sins. The following chapters contain a severe rebuke for political alliances with pagan nations (Chs. 7–12). That fatal policy was to result in pitiless invasion and devastation by hostile armies. However, the prophet predicts the destruction of the nearer enemies, Ephraim and Syria, the defeat of the more distant hosts of Assyria, and the future glory of Jerusalem. This deliverance and glory would not be secured by political intrigue but by divine power symbolized in the name of One who would be called "Immanuel," which means "God is with us."

The section opens with an account of a dramatic episode. This was the meeting of Isaiah with Ahaz the king. Both the king and his people were terrified by the invading armies of Syria and (Northern) Israel:

His heart and the heart of his people shook
as the trees of the wood are moved with the wind
   (Ch. 7:1–2).

In his desperation Ahaz determines to apply to Assyria for aid. This policy would result in disaster.

Judah would become a mere vassal of the great empire.

Isaiah is sent to assure the king of deliverance from Syria and Israel if he will trust in the Lord. However, the prophet is accompanied by his son Shear-jashub (whose name means "a remnant shall return"). The very name was to symbolize a warning. If Ahaz will not trust in the Lord, then a greater calamity would fall upon the people. The Assyrian would be the instrument of such a destruction of Judah that only a mere remnant would escape.

As for the kings of Syria and Israel, whose approach has caused Ahaz such terror, they may be despised. They are mere "smoldering stumps of two firebrands"; they are burned out, impotent. While they are the "heads" of their two nations, the head of Judah is Jerusalem and the head of Jerusalem is the Lord. The trust of the people must be in Him:

> If ye will not believe,
>   Surely ye shall not be established (vs. 3–9).

A second time Isaiah appeals to the king. He offers to present any kind of a "sign" that the king may name, or any possible proof, that God will fulfill His promise to defeat Syria and Israel. Ahaz makes an evasive reply. He already has determined on the desperate course of applying for aid to Assyria. Therefore, with feigned piety he answers: "I will not ask, and I will not put the Lord to the test."

Isaiah bursts out with indignant rebuke:

> Hear then, O house of David! Is it a small thing for you to weary men, that you weary my God also? There-

fore the Lord himself shall give you a sign. Behold, a virgin shall conceive, and bear a son, and shall call his name Immanuel.

Matthew finds the complete fulfillment of this promise in the miraculous birth of our Lord, and in the name He was to bear (Matt. 1:18–25).

Yet the "sign" promised to Isaiah was not merely in the name but in the experience of the child whose age was to mark the time of the divine intervention.

He shall eat curds and honey when he knows how to refuse the evil and choose the good. For before the child knows how to refuse the evil and choose the good, the land before whose two kings you are in dread will be deserted.

Here "curds and honey" are marks of poverty and not of abundance. The land will be so far desolated that instead of bread and meat, the inhabitants must live on the products of an impoverished pastoral people.

Thus the "sign" has a twofold meaning. God will so manifest His power that Syria and Israel will be destroyed, but Judah will be laid desolate by these enemies. The mad policy of Ahaz will issue in a calamity greater than any in the previous history of the land.

The Lord will bring upon you and upon your people and upon your father's house such days as have not come since the day that Ephraim departed from Judah—the king of Assyria (vs. 10–17).

To a description of this tragedy the remaining verses of the chapter are devoted. Isaiah paints five vivid word pictures. The hosts of Assyria are compared to swarms of poisonous insects, which come from Egypt as well as Assyria, since Ahaz has planned to seek help from both those countries (vs. 18, 19).

Again, Assyria is compared to a razor which Ahaz had intended to use against his enemies, but which the Lord is to employ to the disgrace and distress of Judah (v. 20).

The land is to be so devastated that of the former flocks and herds hardly enough will be left to keep alive the small remnant of the people (v. 21).

The beautiful vineyards and gardens of Judah will be desolate wastes of thorns and briars, where men will hunt wild beasts in the thickets, and seek pasture for cattle (vs. 23–25).

To attest the truth of his prophecy, Isaiah is directed to erect, in a public place, a large tablet on which he is to inscribe in bold letters:

TO MAHER-SHALAL-HASH-BAZ

and he is to summon two prominent citizens as witnesses that this is the work of Isaiah (Ch. 8:1, 2).

Furthermore, this name (which means, "The spoil speedeth, the prey hasteth") is to be given to his second son, yet to be born, "for before the child knows how to cry 'My father' or 'My mother,' the wealth of Damascus and the spoil of Samaria will be carried away before the king of Assyria." Thus the calamity was near; and Isaiah proceeds to describe the terrifying invasion of the Assyrian hosts. It will be like the rush of an irresistible flood.

Nor was Judah to escape:

Because this people have refused the waters of Shiloah that flow gently [i.e., have been unwilling to trust in the silent gracious providences of God] and melt in fear before Rezin and the son of Remaliah: therefore, behold, the Lord is bringing up against them the waters of the River, mighty and many, the king of Assyria and all his glory; and it will rise over all its channels and go over all its banks; and it will sweep on into Judah, it will overflow and pass on, reaching even to the neck [i.e., the chief city, Jerusalem] and its outspread wings will fill the breadth of your land, O Immanuel.

Yet Isaiah is not in despair. Judah is "Immanuel's land." A divine pledge has been given and embodied in the name of that child. A "remnant" is sure to be saved. In that confidence the prophet flings out his word of defiance against all enemies:

Speak the word, and it will not stand, for God is with us (Ch. 8:1–10).

Isaiah is divinely warned against yielding to popular clamor or to the fears of the people. God alone is to be trusted and feared. He will be a "sanctuary," a "protection," for all who turn to Him, but He will be a "stone of offence, and a rock of stumbling" to those who fail to recognize and obey Him (vs. 11–15).

The people will not be persuaded. They accept the fatuous policy of the king. Therefore, the prophet withdraws from public service to the private group of his disciples. He orders them to bind up the scroll of his prophecies for future reference. The prophet will "wait for the Lord" and "will hope in him." He and his children, who bear prophetic names, will be as silent "signs" and "omens" of a brighter day to come (vs. 16–18).

However, now the darkness deepens. As often happens, those who refuse divine revelation become the dupes of charlatans and deceivers. They have recourse to spiritualistic mediums. They turn to the dead to find guidance for the living. The prophet warns them to turn to his inspired teaching and testimony. "If they speak not according to this word surely there is no morning for them." The only hope of a brighter day lies in obedience to the revealed will of God (vs. 19–20).

The night becomes black. Punishment has come. The northern tribes of Zebulun and Naphtali first feel the force of the invasion. The people pass through the land greatly distressed and hungry. They curse their king who cannot help them; they curse God who will not deliver. "They look upward to heaven and downward to the earth, but behold distress and darkness, gloom and anguish, and are driven away into thick darkness" (vs. 21–22).

The prophet cannot stop here. He must look at once to a brighter future:

> The people that walked in darkness
> have seen a great light;
> They that dwell in the land of the shadow of
> death
> upon them hath the light shined.

Matthew finds the truest fulfillment of the prophecy in the earthly ministry of our Lord as He

begins his work in Galilee (Matthew 4:15, 16). It is
not to be supposed that Isaiah had this ministry dis-
tinctly in mind. He was, however, looking for a
brighter age in which there would be no hunger or
oppression, and when all the implements of war would
be burned in fire. This age would be introduced by a
Messiah, an ideal King, predicted as "Immanuel,"
who was to bear a still more marvelous title:

> For unto us a child is born,
>   unto us a son is given:
> and the government shall be upon his shoulder:
>   and his name shall be called
> *Wonderful Counselor, Mighty God,*
>   *Everlasting Father, Prince of Peace.*

Of His righteous and just rule there would be no
end. Such a consummation would be due to no power
or achievement of men. It would have its source in
the grace of God and in His jealous love for His people:

> The zeal of the Lord of Hosts will perform this
>   (Ch. 9:1–7).

Before the ideal kingdom can be established there
are foes to be overcome. Therefore, Isaiah announces
the destruction of Northern Israel (Ch. 9:8–10:4) and
the defeat of Assyria (Ch. 10:5–34).

The prophecy relating to Israel is embodied in
an artistic poem of four stanzas, each ending with the
refrain:

> For all this his anger is not turned away,
>   but his hand is stretched out still.

In spite of pride and arrogance, the land will be invaded by enemies, the Syrians from the east and the Philistines from the west,

> And they shall devour Israel with open mouth (vs. 8–12).

The people will suffer defeat and ruthless slaughter because they follow false leaders.

> Neither do they seek the Lord of hosts (vs. 13–17).

Complete civil anarchy will destroy the nation, consumed by jealousies and passions,

> The people shall be like fuel for the fire,
> no man shall spare his brother (vs. 18–21).

The heartless and unjust judges will share the common fate. There will be no one to defend them. They can expect only captivity and death:

> Nothing remains but to crouch among the prisoners
> or fall among the slain.

All warnings and disciplines have failed; judgment must fall (Ch. 10:1–4).

The instrument of punishment is to be the Assyrian. In response to the entreaty of Ahaz he will sweep down and overwhelm Israel. Will he stop there? Like a ravenous beast which has tasted blood he will attack Judah, and the pitiful price for the policy of the king will be paid. The land will be invaded, desolated, despoiled; but when they are under the very walls of Jerusalem disaster falls on the hosts of Assyria and they withdraw to their own country. Judah is to live, but Assyria is to be destroyed. This *defeat* of *Assyria* is recorded in the remaining portion of the chapter (Ch. 10:5–34).

In reality Assyria is merely a "rod" with which God is to punish Judah for her sins. This the conqueror does not understand. He proudly imagines that by his own might and power he has been able "to destroy and to cut off nations not a few." He is heard to boast:

> Shall I not, as I have done unto Samaria and her idols,
>> so do to Jerusalem and her idols? (vs. 5, 11).

However, when the Lord has "performed his whole work" of judgment "upon Zion and Jerusalem," then he will turn and "punish the fruit of the stout heart of the king of Assyria," which fruit includes all his arrogant and cruel words and deeds.

Shall the mere instrument, which the Lord has used, defy the Lord himself?

> Shall the ax vaunt itself over him who hews with it,
>> or the saw magnify itself against him who wields it?
> As if a rod should wield him who lifts it,
>> or as if a staff should lift up itself,
> as if it were not wood!

Therefore famine and fire would destroy the Assyrian host. It would become like a forest in which but a few trees are left standing (vs. 12–19). As to the "remnant of Israel," it will no longer "lean upon him that smote them"—the Assyrian enemy—but will lean upon the Holy One of Israel. Therefore thus saith the Lord:

> Be not afraid of the Assyrian. . . . For in a very little while my anger will be directed to his destruction. . . . And in that day his burden will depart from thy shoulder, and his yoke will be destroyed from thy neck (vs. 20–27).

Then follows a vivid picture of the rapid advance of the Assyrian enemy. Stronghold after stronghold falls, and he stands in defiance before the walls of Jerusalem.

> This very day he will halt at Nob,
>   he will shake his fist at the mount
> of the daughter of Zion.

Then sudden disaster falls, and the Assyrian host like a majestic and stricken forest is cut down and despoiled (vs. 28–34).

The towering cedar has fallen, prostrate, hopeless; but, by way of contrast, "there shall come forth a rod out of the stem of Jesse and a Branch shall grow out of his roots." The royal house of Judah may be cut down, but as an oak it will send forth from its stump a Shoot, even the predicted Immanuel (Ch. 11:1).

The poetic prophecy of *Messiah's reign* (Ch. 11) will find its complete fulfillment in the perfected kingdom of Christ. The ideal king is to rule in *righteousness*:

And the Spirit of the Lord shall rest upon him,
  the spirit of wisdom and understanding,
  the spirit of counsel and might,
  the spirit of knowledge and the fear of the
    Lord. . . .
Righteousness shall be the girdle of his waist,
  and faithfulness the girdle of his loins.

It is to be a reign of peace. Even the fiercest of the lower animals are pictured as living in harmless companionship with helpless children, and all men live in harmony because of the universal knowledge of the Lord:

The wolf shall dwell with the lamb,
  and the leopard shall lie down with the kid
and the calf and the lion and the fatling together,
  and a little child shall lead them. . . .
They shall not hurt or destroy in all my holy
    mountain,
  for the earth shall be full of the
  knowledge of the Lord
  as the waters cover the sea.

The Messiah Himself will be the Centre around whom His own people will gather, and by whom will be attracted the nations of the world:

In that day the root of Jesse shall stand as an
  ensign to the peoples; him shall the nations
    seek,
and his dwelling shall be glorious.

It will be a reign of *restoration* and *release*. There will be a second Exodus, more memorable than that from Egypt:

In that day the Lord will extend his hand yet a second time to recover the remnant which is left of his people.

The most bitter animosities will be put aside, ancient enemies will be subdued. The Lord will open up a way for His returning people

as there was for Israel
when they came up from the land of Egypt (vs. 12–16).

As the deliverance from Egypt was celebrated by Moses' Song of Triumph (Exodus 15), so this prediction of future redemption is followed by a notable psalm of praise (Ch. 12). This psalm may be divided into two strophes of three verses each. The first lines in each case declare what the redeemed people will say when the promises just recorded have been fulfilled:

I will give thanks to thee, O Lord,
   for though thou wast angry with me
      thy anger turned away,
   and thou didst comfort me.
Behold, God is my salvation,
   I will trust, and not be afraid:
      for the Lord God is my strength and my song,
   and he has become my salvation (vs. 1–2).

Then the prophet gives assurance to the people of continual supplies of divine grace:

> With joy you will draw water from the wells of
> salvation (v. 3).
> In that day the yeople will call to one another
> and say:
> Give thanks to the Lord,
>   call upon his name;
> make known his deeds among the nations,
>   proclaim that his name is exalted.
> Sing praises to the Lord, for he has done glori-
> ously;
>   let this be known in all the earth (vs. 4–5).

Then the prophet calls upon Jerusalem to rejoice.

> Shout and sing for joy, O inhabitant of Zion,
>   for great in your midst is the Holy One of
>   Israel (v. 6).

Thus the hymn which ends the "Book of Immanuel" (Chs. 7–12) closes with the divine title which characterizes all the prophecies of Isaiah: "The Holy One of Israel" (Ch. 12:6).

4. THE DOOM OF THE NATIONS [CHS. 13–23]

The record of ten "burdens," or prophecies of judgment, may seem to form a sudden transition from the prediction of glory (Ch. 11) and the psalm of praise (Ch. 12). However, it will be remembered that already the fall of Assyria has been pronounced (Ch. 10), and the judgment on other nations which have been related to Judah is due to their defiance of divine law and will issue in the ultimate deliverance of the people of God. These "burdens" are arranged in two series of five prophecies each (Chs. 13 to 20 and 21 to 23).

The first of each series concerns *Babylon*. This great city and its vast empire is a type and a symbol, in the Old Testament and the New, of *cruel and ruthless imperialism*. The prophecy opens with a summons addressed by the Lord to the enemies of Babylon who are mustered as agents of divine judgment. The sound of their approach is called "a tumultuous noise of the kingdom of nations gathered together." The Babylonians are paralyzed with fear and amazement. "The day of the Lord is upon them, cruel both with wrath and fierce anger, to lay the land desolate." In bold figures of speech a worldwide visitation is pictured as culminating on Babylon. The whole order of nature is disturbed; the heavenly bodies are darkened and the earth is convulsed. The city is captured with savage cruelties. The Medes, whose barbarities were proverbial, are expressly mentioned as the agents of destruction; "and Babylon, the glory of kingdoms, the beauty of the Chaldees' excellency, shall be as when God overthrew Sodom and Gomorrah." The site of the city shall not be frequented even by wandering Arabs or by shepherds with their flocks, but only by wild beasts of the desert, the presence of which shall be a symbol of absolute and abiding desolation (Ch. 13).

The divine purpose of God in the destruction of Babylon has been the deliverance and restoration of His own people. Thus the prophecy continues: "The Lord will have mercy on Jacob and will yet choose

Israel, and set them in their own lands." He will give
them rest from their sorrow, their fear and their bond-
age (Ch. 14:1–3). They will take upon their lips a
"taunting-song," a parable, a dirge, in which they
exult over their cruel foe (vs. 4–21). "The king of
Babylon," whose fall is pictured here need not be
identified with any particular tyrant. The description
is figurative, imaginative. It includes the features of
arrogance and pride and cruelty which characterize a
godless tyrant, and expresses with incomparable vivid-
ness the vanity of human pomp and power:

> How hath the oppressor ceased!
> The golden city ceased!
> He that ruled the nations in anger
> Is persecuted and none hindereth.
> The whole earth is at rest, and is quiet.

By the boldest play of fancy the spirits of the underworld are seen welcoming in irony the mighty ruler as
he helplessly enters the place of the dead:

> Hell from beneath is moved for thee
>   to meet thee at thy coming:
> it stirreth up the dead for thee,
>   even all the chief ones of the earth;
> it hath raised up from their thrones
>   all the kings of the nations.
> All they shall speak and say unto thee,
>   Art thou also become weak as we?
> art thou become like unto us? . . .
>
> How art thou fallen from heaven,
>   O Lucifer, son of the morning!

> how art thou cut down to the ground,
> which didst weaken the nations!

How insolently had he boasted in the little day of his power:

> For thou hast said in thine heart,
> I will ascend into heaven,
> I will exalt my throne
> above the stars of God:
> I will ascend above the heights of the clouds,
> I will be like the most High.
> Yet thou shalt be brought down to hell,
> to the sides of the pit.
> They that see thee shall narrowly look upon thee,
> and consider thee, saying,
> Is this the man that made the earth to tremble,
> that did shake kingdoms;
> That made the world as a wilderness,
> and destroyed the cities thereof;
> that opened not the house of his prisoners?

Now the imagination turns from the underworld to the deserted field of battle and to the dishonored corpse from which the spirit had fled. In contrast with the burial of Oriental kings is the treatment of this abhorred body.

> All the kings of the nations,
> even all of them,
> lie in glory,
> every one in his own house.
> But thou art cast out of thy grave
> like an abominable branch,

and as the raiment of those who are slain,
   thrust through with a sword,
that go down to the stones of the pit;
   as a carcase trodden under feet.

Nor is there any hope for the future. The members of the royal family are to be destroyed. The scene of former glory is to become desolate: "I will sweep it with the besom of destruction, saith the Lord of Hosts" (vs. 20–23).

Rather abruptly the prophecy turns from the desolation of Babylon to the destruction of the Assyrians (Ch. 14:24–27). The latter event already has been related (Ch. 10). The reference here may indicate that the fulfillment of the one prediction may be a guarantee of the other. Both these empires were alike in their power, their barbarous cruelty, their disregard of divine law and human justice. Both are included in the rule of God and in his purpose "that is purposed upon the whole earth"; and no ruthless tyranny can long continue in a world controlled by a righteous God.

The *Burden of Philistia* is recorded briefly (Ch. 14:28–32). These Philistines were the hereditary enemies of Judah. For their cruelties and idolatries they must expect divine retribution. The temporary relief from the power of an oppressor has led them to rejoice. The joy is premature. A more cruel foe is upon them, and a third; each one more venomous and more cruel than the one from which they have found relief. The poorest of God's people shall find food and shelter but of the Philistines not even a remnant will escape. The entire nation will disappear before the hosts which stream from the north, as the fiery cloud sweeps upon them. Some may seek counsel from the prophet. There is but one answer: Zion stands firm and safe in the protection of the Lord.

"The Burden of Moab" (Chs. 15 and 16) is not without notes of tenderness and pity. The description is sufficiently distressing, with scenes of desolation, anguish, mourning, and the sound of weeping; it is made the more vivid and real by the mention of so many historic places on which the universal disaster has fallen; however, the prophet is overwhelmed with sympathy. He mingles his tears with those of the sufferers whose doom he is required to pronounce:

> Therefore I will weep with the weeping of Jazer
>   for the vine of Sibmah;
> I will water thee with my tears,
>   O Heshbon and Elealeh. . . .
> Therefore my heart moans like a lyre for Moab,
> and my soul for Kirheres (Ch. 16:9, 11).

Another striking feature of the oracle is the call to Moab to renew allegiance to the house of David, and the appeal to Jerusalem to shelter the fugitives of Moab, particularly on the ground of Messianic hope:

> Then a throne will be established in steadfast love
>   and on it will sit in faithfulness
>   in the tent of David
> one who judges and seeks justice
>   and is swift to do righteousness (Ch. 16:1–5).

What stands in the way of escape, of deliverance, of pardon? Only one obstacle:

> We have heard of the pride of Moab,
>> that he is very proud,
> of his arrogance, his pride, and his wrath (Ch. 16:6).

It may be well to ask how far does proud and self-conscious nationalism stand in the way of progress and peace among the peoples of the world today?

"The Burden of Damascus" and the prophecy against Samaria form a single "Oracle" (Ch. 17). Syria is named from its capital city, Damascus; and Northern Israel from its capital, Samaria. These two kingdoms had united against Judah. It was an unholy alliance. Israel had forgotten its godly heritage, and depended for help on a pagan power. Both kingdoms would be overwhelmed in a common disaster as the hosts of Assyria assail them from the north. The destruction will be complete, as when a field is stripped of its grain or an olive tree is shaken to bring down the fruit; only the most pitiful gleanings will remain. In their despair the people will turn to God, and not trust in their idol images:

> In that day shall men look unto their Maker,
> and their eyes shall have respect to the Holy One
>> of Israel; . . .
> and they will not have respect to what their own
> fingers have made (Ch. 17:7).

Yet it will be too late. Destruction is upon them. They must suffer the penalty for their impiety and rebel-

lion. This is the very explanation of their fall; and
this is the message for nations of the present day:

> For thou hast forgotten the God of thy salvation,
> and have not remembered the rock of thy refuge
> (v. 10).

When the heartless Assyrians have served as the
instrument of divine displeasure, the time of their retribution will come. They will sweep down upon
Judah like a flood or a tempest, but in a single night
their hosts will be overwhelmed by disaster:

> The nations roar like the roaring of many waters,
> but he will rebuke them, and they will flee far
> away,
> chased like chaff on the mountains before the
> wind,
> and whirling dust before the storm.
> At evening time, behold, terror!
> Before morning, they are no more!
> This is the portion of those who despoil us,
> and the lot of those who plunder us (vs. 13, 14).

The address to *Ethiopia* (Ch. 18) is not termed a
"Burden," as it is essentially a message of cheer. Distressed by the reported approach of Assyria, the Ethi-
opian king is sending messengers down the Nile in
papyrus boats, and seeking to arouse the nations to an
alliance for common defense. Isaiah bids the messengers return to their "land of whirring wings," to
their nation "tall and smooth," to their "people feared
near and far," "whose land the rivers divide." He summons all the inhabitants of the world to look "when

a signal is raised," to hear "when a trumpet is blown."
For the Lord is to act unhasting and unresting. He is
to "quietly look" from "his dwelling." He is silently
to thwart the fierce assault of Assyria on Judah at the
very hour when the Assyrian seems ready to succeed:

> Before the harvest, when the blossom is over,
>   and the flower becomes a ripening grape,
> he will cut off the shoots with pruning hooks,
>   and the spreading branches he will hew away
>   (v. 5).

Impressed by so great a marvel of divine providence, the Ethiopians will send their gifts "to Mount
Zion, the place of the name of the Lord of hosts."

The *"Oracle concerning Egypt"* (Ch. 19) consists
of two strikingly constrasted parts, a warning (vs. 1–
17) and a promise (vs. 18–25). The ancient empire,
wholly devoted to idolatry, and vainly boasting its
wisdom, is threatened with civil discord and anarchy,
succeeded by cruel tyranny:

> I will give over the Egyptians into the hand
>   of a cruel lord;
> and a fierce king will rule over them,
>   says the Lord, the Lord of hosts (v. 4).

This will be followed by physical disaster:

> "And the waters of the Nile will be dried up,"

which represents the failure of all that was essential to
national life. In the hour of dire need "the wise counselors of Pharaoh" can give no guidance and no relief (vs. 1–17).

However, when severely chastened, Egypt will

turn from its idols, and "swear allegiance to the Lord of hosts," and "there will be an altar to the Lord in the midst of the land of Egypt." More marvelous still, Assyria and Egypt, two chief oppressors of Israel, will unite with Israel in worship.

In that day shall Israel be the third with Egypt and with Assyria, even a blessing in the midst of the land: whom the Lord of hosts shall bless, saying, Blessed be Egypt my people, and Assyria the work of my hands, and Israel mine inheritance (vs. 18–25).

No more remarkable missionary passage can be found in all the prophecies of the Old Testament.

Turning from the peaceful dream of an ideal future, the prophet reverts to realities of the darker present. He recounts a personal experience which concerns the defeat and disgrace of the kingdoms of Egypt and Ethiopia. Instead of a prophetic speech, he is bidden to perform a symbolic act. Removing his outer garments, barefoot and in the garb of a prisoner, he appears in public. "And the Lord said, So shall the king of Assyria lead away the Egyptians prisoners, and the Ethiopians captives."

The message is intended first of all for the leaders of Judah. A party opposed to Isaiah is continually advising the king to turn to Egypt for help against Assyria. This symbolic action indicates the folly of such a course. It is a rebuke to those who would substitute political intrigue for faith in God. The people of Judah "shall be afraid and ashamed of Ethiopia their expectation and of Egypt their glory," and they will say in that day, "Behold, this is what happened to those in whom we hoped and to whom we fled for help to be delivered from the king of Assyria! And we, how shall we escape?" (Ch. 20).

In the *Burden against Babylon* (Ch. 21:1–10, R.S.V.) the great city is called "the wilderness of the sea," as situated beyond the desert and beside the broad Euphrates. The picture of its fall is so appalling as to fill the prophet with distress. He sees the enemy approach "as whirlwinds in the south sweep on." "A stern vision is told to me," cries the prophet, "the plunderer plunders, and the destroyer destroys" (vs. 1, 2).

The Medes and the Persians are called to assault the city. At the sight of their approach the prophet is so "bowed down" that he "cannot hear," so dismayed that he "cannot see" (v. 3).

> They prepare the table, they spread the rugs,
>> they eat, they drink. Arise, O princes,
>> oil the shield (v. 5).

The prophet stands as a watchman to receive the report of the disaster. He is heard to cry as with the loud voice of a lion:

> Fallen, fallen is Babylon;
>> and all the graven images of her gods
>> he has shattered to the ground (v. 9).

The closing lines of the "Burden" are addressed to Judah. The destruction of Babylon would be for the deliverance of the people of God, and for their comfort the prophecy is uttered:

> O my threshed and winnowed one,
>> what I have heard from the Lord of hosts,
>> the God of Israel, I announce to you (v. 10).

The *Oracle concerning Edom,* or Seir, is said to be "the only gentle utterance in the Old Testament on Israel's hereditary foe." The country here is called "Dumah" ("silence") to picture its solitude and desolation. Out of the dark night of calamity comes a voice, asking how much of the night remains. The reply of the prophet is sympathetic, but disappointing: "Day will dawn but a night will follow." If one desires, the appeal may be repeated, but there is no promise of explanation or reply. In Christian poetry these lines are quoted in a message of cheer. However, in this "Burden" no star of hope appears. The only answer is "Dumah," silence.

> One is calling to me from Seir,
>> Watchman, what of the night?
>> Watchman, what of the night?
> The watchman says:
>> Morning comes, and also the night.
>> If you will inquire, inquire;
>> come back again (Ch. 21:11–12).

"The Burden upon Arabia" pictures its distress when the Assyrian hosts pour down those dusty, dreary, distant roads. The caravans of merchants are turned from their usual routes of travel to hide in the thickets, while food and drink are brought to the fugitives by the inhabitants of Tema.

> For they fled away from the swords,
>> from the drawn sword,
> and from the bent bow,
>> and from the grievousness of war (v. 15).

Yet flight, or aid to the fugitives, will soon be shut off.

Within a year . . . all the glory of Kedar shall fall; and the residue of the number of archers, the mighty men of the children of Kedar, shall be diminished: for the Lord God of Israel hath spoken (Ch. 21:13–17).

From these prophecies of punishment upon the surrounding nations, Isaiah now turns to his own people. He pronounces *"The Burden of the Valley of Vision,"* by which phrase he designates Jerusalem, the very home of prophecy. The chapter (22) is in two portions: first, a rebuke of the people for their spirit of frivolity and recklessness in the hour of hopeless crisis (vs. 1–14), and, second, the denunciation of Shebna, the court treasurer (vs. 15–25).

The foolish hope of help from Egypt has failed. The Egyptian armies had been defeated and the victorious hosts of Assyria were at the gates of Jerusalem. The city, in the forced gaiety of despair, or in mad self-confidence, was given over to revelry; but the prophet, seeing the rulers in flight and the desperate perils of a siege, is dismayed. He refuses to be comforted:

> Therefore I said,
> Look away from me,
> let me weep bitter tears;
> do not labor to comfort me,
> for the destruction of the daughter
> of my people.

He beheld the ominous approach of the enemy; he heard the crash of the battering rams against the walls; he saw the surrounding valleys filled with hostile chariots; he portrayed the frenzied attempts to prepare the city for the siege. Every expedient had been tried except one, the supreme one, namely, turning to God for help:

> But you looked not to him who did it,
>> to the Lord who created the city and was bringing
>> his judgments upon it,
> nor have regard for him who planned it long
>> ago.

The threatened disaster was a call to repentance and prayer, "to weeping and to mourning," but the senseless people gave themselves to banqueting and feasting. They cast off all moral restraints, and were saying in the very hour of doom: "Let us eat and drink, for tomorrow we die."

For such an attitude of mind there is no place for pardon.

It was revealed in mine ears by the Lord of hosts, Surely this iniquity shall not be purged from you till ye die, saith the Lord God of hosts.

However, Isaiah will not despair. In the darkest hour he cherishes hope of a repentant and redeemed "remnant." This hope is voiced by two historic incidents more eloquently than by any words of prophecy. They express the assurance that Jerusalem can expect a more stable government.

Shebna, called "the treasurer" or the "steward of the palace," a position of power and influence, is to be deposed. He apparently was an ostentatious foreigner who had risen to leadership of the party opposed to Isaiah, which sought for an alliance with Egypt. He had displayed his vanity by appearing in public in stately chariots, and by building for himself a pretentious tomb. He was a type of the frivolous, reckless, sensual princes who had been in control of the city.

Isaiah predicts that the Lord will "whirl him round and round and throw him like a ball into a wide land," and there shall he die.

His high station will be taken by Eliakim, a man who would be "a father to the inhabitants of Jerusalem and to the house of Judah." His authority is described by words afterwards used in predicting the power of the Son of God:

I will place on his shoulder the key of the house of David; he shall open, and none shall shut; and he shall shut, and none shall open (v. 22; Rev. 3:7).

Changing the figure of speech, the prophet declares:

I will fasten him like a nail in a sure place, and he will become a throne of honor to his father's house.

The figure of a "nail" driven "in a sure place" is continued, to convey, for the new ruler, a warning. It may be possible to hang on a nail a weight greater than the nail can support. All the family and relatives of a man in office may come to so depend on him, and so impose upon him, as to cause his downfall. This, in spite of his high character and good intentions, may be the fate of Eliakim:

In that day, says the Lord of hosts, the nail that was fastened in a sure place will give way; and it will be cut down and fall, and the burden that was upon it will be cut off, for the Lord has spoken (v. 25).

"The Burden of Tyre" (Ch. 23) is a solemn warning to men and to nations, lest they barter for material wealth the highest moral and spiritual benefits which life may afford. It is a severe rebuke of the *mercenary spirit* associated with the city which had established a commercial empire extending over the known world.

As the oracle opens, the merchant ships returning from distant Spain learn, as they reach Cyprus, that Tyre has fallen and no harbors await them. The land which has been enriched by the commerce of the seas is dumb with terror. Zidon can be of no help. The news of the disaster brings anguish to Egypt. The people of Phœnicia are urged to seek refuge in their distant colonies.

Tyre, the "exultant" ancient city, "the bestower of crowns," "whose merchants were princes," "whose traders were the honored of the earth," is to be destroyed, for the Lord of hosts has purposed it. He has said:

> Thou shalt no more rejoice
> > O oppressed virgin daughter of Sidon;
> arise, pass over to Cyprus,
> > even there shalt thou have no rest (v. 12).

The fate of the Chaldeans at the hands of Assyria may be a warning to Tyre of what her own fate may be:

> Wail, O ships of Tarshish,
> > for your stronghold is laid waste.

The close of the oracle is marked by mystery and surprise. The general meaning, however, seems to be clear. "At the end of seventy years the Lord will visit Tyre." A large measure of her wealth and commercial prosperity will be destroyed, but not her queenly dignity among the nations. The unexpected prediction which follows is this:

Her merchandise and her hire will be dedicated to the Lord, . . . and will supply abundant food and durable clothing for those who dwell before the Lord (v. 18).

This at least is true: The profits from commercial enterprise can be devoted to the work of the Lord and nobly employed in the support of His servants.

5. THE DAY OF THE LORD [CHS. 24 TO 27]

The "burdens" pronounced on the surrounding nations now reach a climax in predicted judgments on the whole earth. The purpose of these divine visitations is the deliverance and glorious destiny of the people of God.

The language is figurative and poetic. It is not possible to discern any specific events or to distinguish any particular times. Thus in *Chapter 24* the "world" and the "earth" are terms equivalent to the "land," and the description is that of the desolation and ultimate restoration of Judah and Jerusalem. The judgment which falls is universal and on all classes of society. It is due to sin and iniquity (vs. 1–12).

The small remnant that have escaped "will lift up their voice" in distant lands to praise the Lord for their deliverance (vs. 13–15). Yet songs of joy are premature. Flood and earthquake and convulsions of nature picture the judgments upon the guilty city, but the final issue is to be deliverance for the people and the reign of the Lord. Before the splendor of that reign all lesser powers will fade:

Then the moon will be confounded and the sun ashamed; for the Lord of hosts will reign on Mount Zion and in Jerusalem (vs. 16–23).

The prophet identifies himself with his people and places in their mouths a song of thanksgiving (ch. 25):

O Lord, thou art my God;
I will exalt thee, I will praise thy name (v. 1).

Deliverance from a powerful enemy has been secured, and for this thanks are being given:

For thou hast made the city a heap,
the fortified city a ruin.

The Lord has been a Protector to his own people:

Thou hast been a stronghold to the poor,
a stronghold to the needy in his distress
a shelter from the storm and a shade from the
heat.

In the holy city He has prepared a bountiful banquet. He invites all the nations to partake of the blessings He offers:

On the mountain the Lord of hosts will make
for all people a feast of fat things.

He will destroy the veil of spiritual blindness that is "spread over all nations." "He will swallow up death in victory; and the Lord God will wipe away tears from off all faces." Hereditary and inveterate enemies such as Moab will be subdued.

> And it shall be said in that day, Lo, this is our
>   God;
> we have waited for him, and he will save us: this
>   is the
> Lord; we have waited for him, we will be glad and
>   rejoice
> in his salvation (Ch. 25:1–12).

Looking forward to a great day of deliverance, the people of God are heard singing another song:

> We have a strong city;
>   Salvation will God set up
>   as walls and bulwarks.
> Open the gates, that the righteous nation
>   which keeps faith may enter in.
> *Thou wilt keep him in perfect peace,*
>   *whose mind is stayed on thee,*
>   *because he trusteth in thee.*
> Trust ye in the Lord for ever:
>   for the Lord God is an everlasting Rock"
>   [a Rock of Ages] (Ch. 26:1–4).

The prophet pleads that the Lord will show His power against the enemies of Judah,

> For when thy judgments are in the earth,
>   the inhabitants of the world learn righteous-
>   ness (vs. 5–9).

In contrast with the inability of His people to save themselves, is the promise of God's power and purpose to give them new life:

> Thy dead shall live, with my dead body shall
>   they rise.
> O dwellers in the dust, awake and sing for joy
>   (vs. 10–19).

Such words find their real fulfillment in the life and immortality brought to light in the Gospel, and in the glorious consummation of Christian hope. Yet the primary application is national and spiritual; it is like the vision of the Valley of Dry Bones (Ezekiel 57:1–14); it is the restoration and "receiving" of Israel, which Paul calls "life from the dead" (Rom. 11:15).

Yet the time of this deliverance and rejoicing has not come. Severe discipline and terrifying judgments must precede. Therefore the people are exhorted to wait a little longer in the solitude of prayer, until God's punishments have fallen on the guilty nations:

> Come, my people, enter your chambers,
>   and shut your doors behind you;
> hide yourselves for a little while
>   until the wrath is past.
> For behold, the Lord is coming
>   forth out of his place
> to punish the inhabitants of the earth (vs.
>   20, 21).

The enemies upon whom judgment was to be visited are symbolized by monsters, whom the Lord would "punish" with His "strong sword." Probably the nations so designated were Assyria and Babylon and Egypt (Ch. 27:1).

On the other hand, God would care for His people as for "a pleasant vineyard":

> I, the Lord, am its keeper;
>   every moment I water it.
> Lest anyone harm it,
>   I guard it night and day.

Hostile nations would be as "thorns and briers" before the avenging fire of the Lord. They should seek His forgiveness and make peace with him. God's vineyard would flourish:

> Israel shall blossom and put forth shoots.
>   and fill the whole world with fruit (Ch.
>   27:2–6).

The punishments by which His people are to be disciplined are very light in comparison with those visited upon their enemies. If the nation will turn from its idolatry, it will be pardoned, and "the guilt of Jacob will be expiated"; but the fortified city of the enemies shall be made desolate,

> A habitation deserted and forsaken, like the wilderness. . . . He who made them will not have compassion on them, he that formed them will show them no favor (Ch. 27:7–11).

The exiles of Israel, however, are to be carefully gathered as a precious harvest; or, as by the sound of a great trumpet, they are to be summoned from distant lands to "come and worship the Lord on the holy mountain at Jerusalem" (Ch. 27:12, 13).

6. THE BOOK OF WOES [CHS. 28 TO 33]

At a time when the whole country was about to be invaded by the Assyrians, and when Judah was placing a fatuous dependence on Egypt for help, Isaiah delivers a series of prophetic warnings or "woes."

First to be mentioned is Samaria, the proud capital of Israel's northern kingdom. Her drunken politicians will have no power to stay the "destroying storm." They "shall be trodden under feet," and their beautiful city "shall be a fading flower" or as early fruit which quickly will be devoured. Yet to the faithful remnant "the Lord of hosts" will bring deliverance, and will be "for a crown of glory, and for a diadem of beauty" (Ch. 28:1–6).

Furthermore, the priests and prophets of Judah, by their drunkenness and debauchery, are incapacitated for service. They insolently mock the prophet as one who is fitted only to teach babes. His tiresome repetitions of warnings and rebukes are like lessons to infants:

Precept upon precept, precept upon precept,
    line upon line, line upon line,
  here a little, there a little.

To them the prophet replies, if they are not willing to accept the "rest" and peace which God offers,

He will speak to them by the barbarous tongue of the invaders. With a few simple words, "line upon line," these will give military orders which will result in slaughter and destruction.

The people felt secure against death, relying upon the "falsehood" and "lies" of their foreign alliances. Safety could be found only by turning to the Lord. He was laying in Zion a "sure foundation." One "who believes will not be in haste," i.e., to seek for human expedients and deliverances. This reference to "a tried stone, a precious corner-stone, a sure foundation," was to find its future fulfillment in the person of Christ (Rom. 9:33; Eph. 2:20; I Peter 2:6, 7).

For the present, however, a storm would overwhelm the faithless rulers, who meanwhile would find no comfort or rest in their political expedients. It could be said of their situation: "The bed is too short to stretch oneself on it, and the covering too narrow to wrap oneself in it." A severe chastisement would fall "from the Lord God of hosts upon the whole land."

Yet the mercy and care of the Lord was illustrated by a pertinent parable taken from the practices of agriculture. As the farmer plows only at certain seasons, and as he uses various processes of threshing, according to the character of the grain, so God's judgments are for certain times, and His chastisement proportioned to the needs of his people (Ch. 28:7–29).

Isaiah pronounces a severe prophecy against *Jerusalem* under the mystical title of "Ariel" (Ch. 29:1). This term is understood to mean "the hearth of God." Accordingly, "it shall be to me like an

Ariel" might mean that the city would become like a "hearth" on which the fire of God's judgment would be kindled (vs. 2–4). In the near future Jerusalem would be besieged and humbled. Yet deliverance would come. A sudden catastrophe would fall upon the city and overwhelm the enemy. Those that "fought against Ariel" would fade away as "a dream, a vision of the night" (vs. 5–8). The people will suffer chastisement because of spiritual stupor which makes the message of Isaiah like a closed book. This condition is due to a long period of religious formalism and hypocrisy.

> Because this people draw near with their mouth
>> and honor me with their lips,
>> while their hearts are far from me" (v. 13).

Therefore judgment must fall. It will rebuke the proud rulers:

> The wisdom of their wise men shall perish,
>> and the discernment of their discerning men
>> shall be hid.

They had acted as though God was ignorant of their political plots, and as if the Creator could not control the creatures He had made. Strange perversity!

> You turn things upside down! (vs. 9–16).

Yet there would be a reversal. The mercy and love of God would not fail. After punishment, restoration would follow. The very face of nature, as well as the hearts of men, will be changed. Spiritual sight and hearing will be restored. "The meek shall obtain fresh joy," and the "poor among men shall exult." The "ruthless" invader "shall come to nought" and "all who watch to do evil shall be cut off" (vs. 17–21).

Jacob is fancied as no longer ashamed of his children, but as rejoicing when he sees them "sanctify the Holy One of Jacob" and "stand in awe of the God of Israel" (vs. 22–24).

Isaiah severely condemns the senseless godless policy of seeking from Egypt help against the Assyrians (Ch. 30). "The protection of Pharaoh" will turn to "shame" and the "shelter of Egypt" to "humiliation." The caravans carrying rich treasures across the dreadful desert are bringing tribute to a nation which will share no profit with Judah. Since Egypt has a reputation for power and cruelty, and yet will give no help, it is properly called a "Rahab," a monster that appears fierce and destructive but, when the time demands action, "sits still" (vs. 1–7).

For the fatal policy of trusting in Egypt the rulers alone were not to blame. The people also were responsible. They did not wish to hear the truth; they would not obey the word of God. It was not an enemy from without, but the spirit within, which threatened to destroy the life of the nations, like "the bulging out of a high wall, about to collapse, whose crash comes suddenly."

There was a way of escape. It could be found in ceasing from their feverish search for political intrigues, and calmly and peacefully trusting in God,

> For thus saith the Lord God,
>   the Holy One of Israel;

In returning and rest shall ye be saved;
in quietness and in confidence shall be your
strength.

But no; such counsel did not appeal to the people. They preferred to trust in the swift horses of Egypt. Isaiah replies: They will ride fast enough, but it will be in retreat. Defeated and deserted, they will be left as a mere warning against godlessness and unbelief (vs. 8–17).

However, the Lord waits to be gracious. The extremity of His people is the opportunity for Him to show His mercy. Isaiah paints an enchanting picture of what that mercy may secure. It is a prophecy of an ideal future, of godliness, of prosperity, of peace and of light (vs. 18–26).

In the immediate present a cruel enemy is on the horizon. The hosts of Assyria are sweeping down like a consuming fire or an overwhelming flood; but in fire or flood, the Lord will be present sifting the nations and exercising His power and restraint. He will deliver his people. "Through the voice of the Lord shall the Assyrians be beaten down." The redeemed will sing in exultation, but the enemy will be consumed as by fire (vs. 27–33).

Isaiah continues to denounce bitterly the foolish alliance with Egypt:

Woe to those who go down to Egypt for help, . . . who trust in chariots because they are many and in horsemen because they are very strong (Ch. 31:1).

The stupid politicians in Jerusalem thought they could meet the hosts of Assyria if only their forces were strengthened by a contingent of Epyptian cavalry. The fatal error of their entire policy lay in refusing to follow the command of the Lord and in supposing that in their intrigues there was more of wisdom. It is still a stratagem of the Tempter to make men believe that the laws of God are less wise than the ways of the world.

Isaiah replies with supreme sarcasm: "He also is wise," there are some things the Lord Himself knows, and His judgments disclose the folly of men: "He will arise against the house of the evildoers. . . . The Egyptians are men, and not God" (vs. 1–3).

The power of the Lord to deliver is pictured in two figures of speech. First, God is compared to a lion which cannot be terrified by the shouting of shepherds but will keep for himself the prey which is his. So will the Lord keep his own holy city. Or as a bird flutters over the nest to protect its young,

> So the Lord of hosts will protect Jerusalem; . . .
> He will spare and rescue it (vs. 4, 5).

Therefore the prophet appeals to the "people of Israel" to turn to the Lord and to put away their idols. If they repent, their enemy will be shattered.

> The Assyrian shall fall by a sword, not of man,
>   and a sword, not of man, shall devour him
>   (vs. 4, 5).

So it came to pass. By no human agency, but by divine intervention, the foe was put to flight (Ch. 37:36).

After describing the destruction of the enemy,

Isaiah again gives a glimpse of the ideal future promised to the people of God. The condition of its blessedness is found in the establishment of just and righteous government:

> Behold a king will reign in righteousness
>> and princes will rule in justice.
> Each will be like a hiding-place from the wind,
>> a covert from the tempest,
> as rivers of water in a dry place,
>> as the shade of a great rock in a weary land
>>> (Ch. 32:1, 2).

Such a condition can exist only when this prophecy has its complete fulfillment and Christ is acknowledged as King of kings and Lord of lords.

Another feature of this ideal is the removal of spiritual blindness and deafness, so that character will be clearly discerned, and moral distinctions no longer confused, and men recognize that God has established an eternal difference between right and wrong (vs. 3–8).

So for the future, but in the immediate present catastrophe awaits. Therefore Isaiah turns to rebuke the women of Jerusalem who on the eve of calamity and crisis are careless and frivolous and complacent. It is predicted that "in little more than a year," "the vintage will fail, the fruit harvest will not come," "the palace will be forsaken, the populous city deserted," and the land become desolate (vs. 9–14).

Such a state will continue until the Spirit of God is poured from on high.

Then justice will dwell in the wilderness,
    and righteousness abide in the fruitful field.
And the effect of righteousness will be peace,
    and the result of righteousness,
        quietness and confidence forever (vs. 16–17).

Yet before such peace, judgment must fall; but the age of blessedness will come, when the whole land shall be fertile and cultivated, abundantly watered by its calmly flowing streams (vs. 15–20).

Again and again Isaiah predicted the overthrow of the Assyrians, but possibly never more vividly than here (Ch. 33). The cruel hordes had destroyed the northern kingdom of Israel and had threatened Judah. By paying an exhorbitant tribute the promise had been secured that Jerusalem would be spared. Then the Assyrian disregarded his treaty and laid siege to the Holy City. In view of this perfidy one can understand the reproach with which Isaiah began his prophecy:

Woe to you, destroyer,
    who yourself have not been destroyed;
you treacherous one,
    with whom none has dealt treacherously (v. 1).

Then the prophet offers his prayer:

O Lord, be gracious to us; we wait for thee.
    Be our arm every morning,
our salvation in the time of trouble (vs. 2–6.)

There is need of prayer; for the "envoys," who thought they had purchased peace "weep bitterly" in disappointment, and "the land mourns and languishes," and the city is too weak to withstand a siege. Then God acts.

> Now I will arise, says the Lord,
>   now I will lift myself up. . . .
> And the people will be as if burned to lime,
>   like thorns cut down, that are burned in the
>   fire.

In a single night the hosts of the enemy are smitten, and the Assyrian army is withdrawn (vs. 10–12).

The whole world will hear of this divine retribution. In Zion itself the godless will be seized with fear. Indeed, all who have witnessed this just judgment of the holy God may well ask: "Who among us can dwell with the devouring fire?"

The answer is given in a memorable description of a man "who walks righteously and speaks uprightly." He will dwell in safety and all his wants will be supplied (vs. 13–16).

To the righteous, who alone will dwell in Zion, comes the promise:

> *Thine eyes shall see the king in his beauty;*
> *they shall behold the land that is very far off.*

The contrast was with a king clothed in sackcloth, and ruling a land hemmed in by foes. The ultimate fulfillment accepted by the followers of Christ pictures the beatific vision of a King in His glory and of "a better country, that is, an heavenly."

But the citizens of ancient Jerusalem, dazed by the suddenness of their deliverance, could think only of yesterday. It all seemed like a dreadful dream—the cruel messengers counting out the ransom money, the rude soldiers insolently defying God and His people in barbarous, unintelligible speech; now all this was gone, and the people were bidden to "look upon Zion." They would see their city was like a tent which could not be moved. Or it was like a fortress surrounded by broad rivers on which streams no hostile vessel would appear. There would be perfect safety because of the presence of the Lord; he was their Judge, their Ruler, their King. The enemy was like a shattered vessel, plundered by those it had come to plunder; but the inhabitants of Jerusalem would enjoy pardon, prosperity, and peace (vs. 17–24).

"The Book of Woes" (Chs. 28–33) here finds its finale in a prophecy of judgment on the whole world (Ch. 34) and in a prediction of the restoration of Israel (Ch. 35). These two chapters likewise may be regarded as an epilogue to the entire collection of prophecies which form the first half of "Isaiah" (Chs. 1–35).

> Come near, ye nations, to hear;
>   and hearken, ye people:
> Let the earth hear, and all that there is therein;
>   the world, and all things that come forth of it.
> For the indignation of the Lord is upon all nations,
>   and his fury upon all their armies:
> he hath utterly destroyed them,
>   he hath delivered them to the slaughter.

In this universal judgment the skies and the stars are pictured as being involved:

> The heaven shall be rolled together as a scroll:
>   and all their host shall fall down.

These figures of speech are borrowed by the New Testament writers (as Matt. 24:29 and Rev. 6:13, 14). They are poetic images depicting sudden, total, and appalling visitation and revolution.

While the whole world is included in the vision of the prophet, he singles out as an example one particular nation, namely, Edom, the inveterate enemy of Judah:

> For my sword shall be bathed in heaven:
>   behold, it shall come down upon Idumea
>   [Edom],
> upon the people I have doomed (Ch. 34:1–5).

The destruction of the people is pictured as the offering of a great sacrifice. The fruitful land is turned into a barren wilderness. Instead of having its former inhabitants, the country is given over to wild and doleful animals, which will dwell in lonely desolation. Their very presence, in future ages, will attest the correctness of this prophecy.

Thus in bold and awful imagery Isaiah proclaims the truth that all who oppose the purposes of God and are the enemies of his people ultimately will be destroyed (vs. 6–17).

In contrast with the prophecy of a verdant land becoming a desert is the picture of a wilderness becoming a region of flowering fields and the glorious home of the redeemed people of God (Ch. 35). This vision of restoration is one which transcends all history and carries the thought beyond any possible earthly fulfillment. It can be applied properly to the return of the Jews from Babylon, or to the Gentiles, called to worship in the mountain of the house of the Lord, or to the experience of every Christian as he journeys onward toward his home in the celestial city.

> The wilderness and the solitary place shall be glad,
>> and the desert shall rejoice, and blossom as the rose,"

and over the fair land shall shine, not merely the light of common day, but its joyful people

> shall see the glory of the Lord,
>> and the excellency of our God" (Ch. 35:1, 2).

To the scattered exiles timidly facing the journey toward Zion come words of encouragement:

> Strengthen ye the weak hands,
>> and confirm the feeble knees.
> Say to them that are of a fearful heart,
>> Be strong, fear not!
>> Behold your God will come; . . .
> He will come and save you (vs. 3, 4).

The presence of the Lord will result in spiritual transformations:

> The eyes of the blind shall be opened,
>> and the ears of the deaf shall be unstopped.

> Then shall the lame man leap as an hart,
> and the tongue of the dumb shall sing.

As they cross the dreary desert glad surprises will await them,

> For in the wilderness shall waters break out
> and streams in the desert.
> And the burning sand [of the mirage] shall become a pool;
> and the thirsty land springs of water.

The Lord will prepare the way before them:

> And a highway shall be there,
> It shall be called the Holy Way;
> For the unclean shall not pass over it.

It will be made perfectly plain before the pilgrims:

> The wayfaring men, even the simple ones,
> shall not lose their way.

It will be perfectly safe, for

> No lion shall be there,
> nor any ravenous beast;
> but the redeemed shall walk there.

This holy highway will surely bring the longing exiles home:

> And the ransomed of the Lord shall return,
> and come to Zion with songs
> and everlasting joy upon their heads:
> they shall obtain joy and gladness,
> and sorrow and sighing shall flee away (vs. 5–10).

II

THE HISTORICAL SECTION

Isaiah 36 to 39

1. THE DEFEAT OF SENNACHERIB [CHS. 36 AND 37]

THE HISTORICAL section forms a link between the first and second portions of the prophecies of Isaiah. It serves as an appendix to the first (Chs. 1 to 35) and an introduction to the second (Chs. 40 to 66). In the earlier chapters Assyria appears as the great foe of Judah; in a later chapter Babylon is the world power which takes Judah captive.

Again and again Isaiah has predicted the overthrow of the Assyrian forces (Ch. 8:5–10; 10:12–19; 30:28–31, etc.). He now records the fulfillment of these prophecies (Chs. 36 and 37). It is a narrative of divine retribution for perfidy and cruelty. Sennacherib, the king of Assyria, had invaded Judah, captured its fortified cities and threatened Jerusalem. On condition that an enormous tribute should be paid, he promised to spare the city; but when he had received the treasure he tore up the treaty and sent a vast army to besiege the Judean capital. The chief representative of the king was called the Rabshakeh. His endeavor was to secure the surrender of Jerusalem without opposition. Near the gates of the city he is met by a delegation from Hezekiah the king. His arrogant address is as crafty as it is insolent. He sends word to the king that it is futile to look for help, either from Egypt or from the Lord. Egypt is a broken reed but will pierce the hand of one who leans upon it; and as for the Lord, He has been displeased by the recent destruction of so many places of worship. The Assyrian does not understand that these were idol shrines, removed by the reforms of Hezekiah. He then resorts to ridicule. He is willing to wager that if he supplies two thousand horses, Hezekiah cannot furnish riders to form a force of cavalry.

He next reminds the people of their unfaithfulness to God. It had been reported to him that Isaiah had declared the invasion of the Assyrian to be a chastisement from the Lord. Therefore in bitter irony this pagan declares: "The Lord said to me, Go up against this land and destroy it."

The envoys of the king then plead with the Rabshakeh to speak in the Syrian language so that the people on the city walls would not understand his threats; but he only replied with a coarse threat of starvation, and with a louder voice, and offered to spare the people for a time if they would surrender, and then to establish them in a more desirable land. The gods of other peoples had not been able to bring deliverance, so it would be futile to expect deliverance from the God of Judah.

The courtiers made no reply, but in deep distress returned to the king to report the threatening message of the Assyrians. In anguish of heart Hezekiah resorts to the temple, and sends a request to Isaiah, earnestly beseeching him to offer "prayer for the remnant that is left," indicating by his very words how desperate the situation had become (Ch. 37:1–4).

Now it is that the heroism of Isaiah reaches its most sublime height. In the darkest hour he has known, when the city is beleagured and helpless, he sends this word to the messengers of the king:

> Say to your master, Thus saith the Lord: Do not be afraid because of the words you have heard, with which the servants of the king of Assyria have reviled me. Behold, I will put a spirit in him, so that he shall hear a rumor, and return to his own land, and I will make him fall by the sword in his own land (vs. 5–7).

The Assyrian king was still at a distance with a large portion of his forces. When the Rabshakeh returns from Jerusalem, Sennacherib is not ready to undertake the destruction of the city. He therefore dispatches a letter in which he repeats the statement that the Lord cannot deliver Judah, as the gods of no nation have been able to withstand the Assyrians (vs. 8–13).

When Hezekiah has received the letter, he goes to the temple and spreads the letter before the Lord, and offers a prayer in which he voices his faith that the gods of the nations were helpless, but the Lord was God of all the kingdoms of the earth, He could not be defied with impunity; his name was at stake in this crisis:

> So now, O Lord our God, save us from his hand, that all the kingdoms of the earth may know that thou alone art the Lord (vs. 14–20).

The answer to this prayer was given through Isaiah in one of the most impressive poems that has come from his pen. It is composed of three stanzas: (1) a taunting song setting forth the certain discomfiture of the Assyrians. They are despised and scorned by the "virgin daughter of Zion": they have boasted of their conquests, mocking the Lord whose plans and providences made those conquests possible, who soon would turn them back to the place from which they came (vs. 21–29); and (2) a short message addressed to Hezekiah designed to strengthen his faith (vs. 30–32); and (3) a definite promise of the deliverance of Jerusalem concluding with these words:

I will defend this city to save it, for my own sake and for the sake of my servant David (vs. 33–35).

Then Isaiah records the fulfillment of this promise:

And the angel of the Lord went forth, and slew a hundred and eighty-five thousand in the camp of the Assyrians. . . . Then Sennacherib, king of Assyria, departed and went home and dwelt at Nineveh. And as he was worshiping in the house of Nisroch his god, his sons slew him with the sword, and escaped into the land of Ararat (vs. 36–38).

The exact nature of the catastrophe which destroyed the Assyrian hosts is not defined. It is commonly supposed that an oriental plague was the instrument of judgment. Nor did his tragic fate overtake the king until after the lapse of years. These events, with minor additions, are recorded in the Second Book of Kings (Chs. 18 and 19). They are repeated here, possibly to attest the truth and exactness of all the prophecies to which they form an appendix, and further to emphasize the realities which form the essential features of those predictions, namely, the certain defeat of the enemies of God and His deliverance and protection of those who put their trust in him.

2. THE SICKNESS AND RECOVERY OF HEZEKIAH. [CH. 38]

Hezekiah, king of Judah, had endeavored faithfully to "walk before the Lord," that is, in obedience and trust, and had sought to reclaim his people from idolatry. It was, therefore, with anguish of heart that he found himself, in the very prime of life, smitten by a fatal disease. For days and nights he suffered the torment of an incurable abscess, but did not despair of recovery, until Isaiah came to him conveying the divine decree: "Thus saith the Lord, Set thine house in order, for thou shalt die and not live."

Then Hezekiah "prayed to the Lord" and "wept bitterly." It was of course a request for recovery. The fragment which is recorded may seem to indicate something of self-righteousness: "Remember, now, O Lord, I beseech thee, how I have walked before thee in faithfulness and with a whole heart, and have done what is good in thy sight." Probably it should be regarded rather as an indication of absolute sincerity and a yearning to know why the calamity had come.

Hardly had Isaiah left the royal palace when he is bidden to return with the message from God: "I have heard your prayer; . . . behold, I will add fifteen years to your life." It is an example of the contingent character of prophetic utterances. Something had occurred. Was it the prayer of the king, or his tears, or something in his heart? In any case, the decree was reversed. The request had been granted, and when the king asked for a sign that he should recover, there came the word: "I will make the shadow cast by the declining sun on the dial of Ahaz turn back ten steps."

As to the miracle which followed, it is useless to inquire the method of a divine action. Those who regard the phenomenon as local, and possibly a refraction of light, such as the afterglow of sunset, are probably nearer the truth than those who insist on some incredible disruption of the solar system. God usually works in accordance with natural causes.

This is well illustrated by the event which followed. A miraculous cure had been promised to the king; but "Isaiah said, Take a lump of figs. And they took and laid it on the boil and he recovered" (II Kings 20:7). Neither the prayer of faith nor the promise of God makes unnecessary the use of means or the employment of human skill (Ch. 38:1-8).

Here Isaiah introduces "the writing of Hezekiah king of Judah, when he had been sick, and was recovered of his sickness" (vs. 9-20). This is a plaintive psalm. It expresses praise, but has overtones of sadness. The writer cannot forget the dreadful experience through which he has passed. He recalls the sudden loss of his royal estate, the long nights of intolerable pain, the vision of the dark and dreary abode of the dead which he was about to enter through the "gates of Sheol." His life had seemed like a moving tent of a shepherd, or like the web of which the threads were being cut from the loom. He remembers his prayer: "O restore me to health and make me live." He knows that the prayer has been heard, that the very suffering had been for his welfare, that life has been preserved, and all sins divinely forgiven and forgotten. Thus the poem can close with a note of triumphant hope:

> The Lord is ready to save me,
>   and we will sing to stringed instruments
> all the days of our life,
>   in the house of the Lord.

3. THE EMBASSY FROM BABYLON [CH. 39]

The illness of Hezekiah is directly connected with the visit of envoys from Babylon. These messengers came ostensibly to bring a present and to congratulate the king on his recovery. A second purpose is stated; it was the desire to learn the nature of the miracle recorded in connection with the recovery of the king (II Chron. 32:31). Probably the real reason for the visit was the desire on the part of the Babylonians to form an alliance with Hezekiah to secure his support against the Assyrians.

In any case, Hezekiah was flattered by the visit and in a spirit of pride and ostentation he showed the envoys all his royal treasures. This was a fatal blunder. Of course the Babylonians would desire to conquer Jerusalem and to seize all its wealth; moreover, it would seem to indicate to those idolators that Hezekiah trusted more to his treasures than to his God.

Isaiah was sent to the king with a stern rebuke and an appalling prophecy:

Behold, the days are coming, when all that is in your house, and that which your fathers have stored up till this day, shall be carried to Babylon: nothing shall be left, says the Lord.

This is one of the most astonishing of all the predictions made by the prophet, because the Assyrians and not the Babylonians were then the great world power. Only divine inspiration would have prompted Isaiah to declare that the Babylonians would be the instrument for the destruction of Jerusalem and the captivity of Judah. Such a prophecy, however, is a fitting conclusion to the first great cycle of prophetic utterances and a prelude to the remaining chapters of the Book, in which Babylon is the tyrant from whom deliverance is sought (Chs. 40–66).

PROPHECIES OF RESTORATION

Isaiah 40 to 66

1. THE POWER OF JEHOVAH [CHS. 40–48]

"Comfort ye, comfort ye my people saith your God."

THESE WORDS sound the keynote of the majestic music which fills the remaining chapters of the book. The message is one of consolation, of pardon, of restoration, of future glory. It is addressed to the Hebrew captives in Babylon; yet finds its ultimate fulfillment in the redeeming work of Christ, and to each of His followers it can bring comfort and consolation and cheer.

The prologue to the prophecies records the words of four celestial voices (Ch. 40:1–11). The first voice brings a message of *pardon*. "Speak ye comfortably to Jerusalem," "tenderly," "to the heart," or "wooingly"; "and cry unto her, that her warfare is accomplished." The "set time of her hard service," the years of captivity are ended. "Her iniquity is pardoned," the bitterest drop of sorrow had been the knowledge that her distress was due to her own transgressions. "She hath received from the Lord's hand double for all her sins," not that suffering is the ground of pardon. Forgiveness is altogether of grace. Yet God does note, in pity, the suffering which men bring upon themselves. The sufferings of Israel have been greater than her sins. Yet now, as ever, God grants forgiveness where there is penitence and faith, So, as believers in Christ "we have redemption through his blood, the forgiveness of sins, according to the riches of his grace" (Eph. 1:7).

The second voice (vs. 3–5) speaks of *providence*. Man must co-operate; There is much that captive Israel must do; resolution, preparation, effort are expected, yet deliverance and restoration must be ascribed to the Lord. "In the wilderness" and across the desert He will prepare a highway. All obstacles will be removed, and "all flesh will see the glory" of God's mighty acts as He leads Israel in triumph back to the land they love.

These words are quoted by John the Baptist in reference to his own mission. "The way of the Lord" which he proclaimed was that of repentance and faith. Men could thus be prepared for the salvation Christ was to offer. "Repent ye," was his plea, "for the kingdom of heaven is at hand."

The third voice (vs. 6–8) contrasts the feebleness and frailty of man with the unfailing *promise* of God. Whether one thinks of the enemies who may oppose, or of the great leaders who have fallen, "all flesh is grass. . . . The grass withereth, the flower fadeth: but the word of our God shall stand for ever." Those who rely on the unfailing word need have no fear; deliverance is sure to come, and there will be a safe journey across the wilderness to the city of God.

The fourth voice (vs. 9–11) proclaims the Good News of the coming of the Lord in *power* as well as grace. Zion is commanded to proclaim these glad tidings to the cities of Judah and to say "Behold your God." Thus the prophet declares:

> Behold, the Lord God comes with might,
>   and his arm rules for him;
> behold, his reward is with him,
>   and his recompense before him.

Yet His coming is not only in might; He will lead His people and establish His kingdom with tenderness and love. "He will feed his flock like a shepherd, he will gather the lambs in his arms."

Thus the "comfort" and encouragement of Israel are based on the revealed power and wisdom of God. He is the Creator of the heavens and the earth; He is the Ruler of all nations.

> Who hath measured the waters in the hollow of
>   his hand,
>   and marked off the heavens with a span,
> enclosed the dust of the earth in a measure
>   and weighed the mountains in scales
>   and the hills in a balance? . . .
> Behold, the nations are as a drop from a bucket,
>   and are accounted as the dust on the scales;
> behold, he taketh up the isles as a very little thing.

With such a God none can compare; but a contrast can be drawn. The prophet, therefore, makes a sarcastic and devastating reference to the manufactured deities of the idolators:

> The workman maketh a graven image,
>   and the goldsmith overlays it with gold,
>   and casts for it silver chains.

He that is too poor for such an offering
   chooseth a tree that will not rot;
He seeks out a skillful workman
   to set up an image that will not move.

How different is

He who sits above the circle of the earth, . . .
who stretches out the heavens like a curtain, . . .
who brings princes to nought,
and makes the rulers of the earth as nothing.

Lift up your eyes on high and see:
   who created these?
He who brings out their host by number,
   calling them all by name;
by the greatness of his might,
   and because he is strong in power
   not one is missing.

Such a sight of the stars is not an argument for the existence of God, but a sacrament in which He imparts to men His power and His grace.

Thus the discouraged and disconsolate captives of Israel must not think that God has forgotten or deserted them. Rather they must wait on the Lord in patient, confident trust and dependence.

Why do you say, O Jacob,
   and speak, O Israel,
My way is hid from the Lord,
and my right is disregarded by my God?
Have you not known? Have you not heard?
The Lord is the everlasting God,
   the Creator of the ends of the earth.

He does not faint or grow weary,
   his understanding is unsearchable.
He gives power to the faint,
     and to him who has no might be increases
      strength.
Even youths shall faint and be weary,
   and young men shall fall exhausted;
but they who wait for the Lord
   shall renew their strength,
they shall mount up with wings like eagles,
they shall run and not be weary,
   they shall walk and not faint.

To soar, to run, to walk—this is no anti-climax; these three may be regarded as forming an ascending scale of increasing difficulty. It may require a fresh impulse of divine grace to mount heavenward on wings of inspired fancy in an hour of spiritual ecstasy, or again to press toward some high goal of moral attainment; but the supreme test of Christian character is found when one can plod along the path of daily duty and across the desert of monotonous toil without praise or prize, yet without complaint, without faltering, without fainting, but with a cheerful and courageous heart.

A long and dreary journey lay before the returning captives as they turned from Babylon toward Jerusalem; yet they were assured of needed strength if they would "wait upon the Lord." So for the people of God today sufficient grace is promised if they trust in Him and move forward on their pilgrim journey toward the City of glory and gold.

In the previous chapter (Ch. 40), the Hebrew captives have been comforted and encouraged by the assurance that while they have been disobedient, God is still their God and they are His people, and as He is the Creator and Ruler of the world, their deliverance is certain if only they will trust in Him.

In this chapter their God is presented as the only One who can predict and control future events, and as He has foretold the appearing of a deliverer such a Saviour will surely come.

The prophecy is phrased under the figures of a trial in court. The nations are summoned to testify to the power of their gods, while Jehovah declares His sole deity. The term by which the nations are described is "islands," the distant "islands of the west," or the "coast-lands," meaning, however, all the peoples of earth.

> Keep silence before me, O islands: . . .
> Let us come near together to judgment (Ch. 41:1).

The Lord speaks first. He bases his claim on the fact that He has predicted that Cyrus is to be the conquerer of Babylon and the deliverer of Israel. The Persian king is not named until in a subsequent prophecy, but the description makes the reference clear:

> Who hath raised up one from the east
> whom victory meets at every step?
> He gives up nations before him,
> so that he tramples kings under foot. . . .
> Who has performed and done this? . . .
> I, the Lord, . . . I am he" (vs. 2–4).

The nations hear the challenge and "are afraid, the ends of the earth tremble." Those who answer the summons try to cheer one another on their way; everyone saying to his brother, "Be of good courage." Those who remain at home make a frantic effort to patch up their dilapidated idols or to manufacture new ones.

> The craftsman encourages the goldsmith,
>> and he who smooths with the hammer him who strikes the anvil,
> saying of the soldering, "It is good";
>> and they fasten it with nails so that it cannot be moved" (vs. 5–7).

It is not so with the people of God. They hear His word of promise:

> *Fear thou not, for I am with thee;*
> *Be not dismayed, for I am thy God;*
> *I will strengthen thee; yea, I will help thee;*
> *Yea, I will uphold thee with the right hand of my*
>> *righteousness.*

All the enemies of Israel will be put to shame, and the nation, now weak and helpless, will be transformed into a "new sharp threshing sledge" to be used as an instrument for punishing the enemies of God.

> And thou shalt rejoice in the Lord,
> and shalt glory in the Holy One of Israel.

As they journey through the desert, God will open for them rivers and fountains of water, and will cover the wilderness with cedars and cypress and pine (vs. 8–20).

After this digression, spoken to comfort the peoples of God, the dialogue is renewed, not now between the Lord and the nations, but between God and the idols.

> Produce your cause, saith the Lord;
>   bring your proofs, saith the King of Jacob.

The proposed test is just; let the gods of the nation predict the future or rightly interpret events of the past. Or let them do anything at all, good or bad; let them show some signs of life. But they were silent, dumb, impotent. The conclusion is inevitable: "Behold, ye are nothing, and your work is nought; he who chooses you is an abomination."

In arresting contrast the Lord is willing to apply to Himself a supreme test of sole deity, namely, the ability to predict the future. He outlines the victorious career of Cyrus the deliverer of Israel, who would "trample" on the princes of Babylon "as on mortar, as the potter treads clay."

While the gods of the heathen were dumb and silent, the Lord declared deliverance to Zion, He "gave to Jerusalem a herald of good tidings." Therefore the Lord pronounces the verdict: There is no one among the idols "who, when I ask, gives an answer, they are all a delusion; their works are nothing; their molten images" are wind and "confusion" (vs. 21–29).

> Behold my servant, whom I uphold,
>   my elect, in whom my soul delighteth;
> I have put my spirit upon him,
>   he shall bring forth justice to the nations.
> He shall not cry, nor lift up,
>   nor cause his voice to be heard in the street.

A bruised reed shall he not break,
   and a smouldering wick shall he not quench;
He shall bring forth judgment faithfully.
   He shall not fail nor be discouraged
   till he hath established judgment upon the
      earth;
   and the isles shall wait for his law (Ch. 42:1–
   4).

Thus Isaiah introduces the most majestic and mysterious Figure which appears in the pages of his prophecy. This *"Servant of Jehovah"* refers, first of all, to Israel; then, more specifically, to the believing, purified "remnant" of the nation; but definitely and supremely to the coming Messiah and Saviour. Matthew (Ch. 12:18–21) quotes this entire paragraph, and declares that it was fulfilled in the ministry of our Lord Jesus Christ. The nature of this ministry is described as the bringing forth of "judgment." This last word is a rather misleading translation. The original term is quite divorced from the conception of a legal verdict, or of social justice, or of national honor. It refers to the law of God, or the summary of all His requirements and has been helpfully defined as "true religion." The high calling of Israel had been to make God and His redeeming grace known to all the world. The nation had failed; but a Redeemer was to come who would fulfill this glorious task. In his ministry He would show a spirit of meekness, of gentleness and of undaunted perseverance. He would be sustained by divine power and would be "for a light to the Gentiles, to open the blind eyes, to bring out the prisoners from the prison, and them that sit in darkness out of the prison house" (vs. 5–9). In such a ministry all the followers of Christ may have a share; but they must show His spirit of sympathy and gentleness, His matchless courage and His dependence on the sustaining power of God (Acts 26:17, 18).

The prophecies of the redeeming work of God evoke a *hymn of praise* (Ch. 42:10–17). The joyful promise is proclaimed that the Lord Himself is to go forth "as a mighty man," and "shall prevail against his enemies," and deliver Israel. He will lead His people back across the barren wilderness, and utterly discomfit all those "that trust in graven images."

However, Israel is not yet prepared to have a part in this ministry of grace. A spiritual renewal is necessary. The nation is still "blind" and "deaf." There is a certain stubborness in its unbelief. Severe punishment has been suffered during years of exile and captivity. Israel is still "a people robbed and spoiled, snared in holes and hid in prison houses." They now need to understand the meaning of this discipline and the conditions of deliverance, of restoration, of divine fellowship and of spiritual service (vs. 8–25).

In spite of the blindness and deafness of Israel, the prophet predicts the coming salvation. This is phrased in words which have brought comfort and cheer to the people of God through all generations down to the present day:

Fear not, for I have redeemed thee,
 I have called thee by thy name; thou art mine.

> *When thou passeth through the waters,*
>   *I will be with thee;*
> *and through the rivers, they shall not overflow*
>   *thee;*
> *when thou walkest through the fire,*
>   *thou shalt not be burned;*
> *neither shall the flame kindle upon thee*
>   (Ch. 43:1, 2).

Thus Israel is to be redeemed even at the cost of the richest of ancient nations; at least, mention is made of Egypt, of Ethiopia, of Seba. The scattered exiles are to be gathered "from the ends of the earth" (vs. 3–7).

After this promise, a challenge is given to "all the nations." It is again in the form of a trial at court (as in 41:1–4). Can any one of the nations, or their gods, produce evidence that they had known the course of human history? Evidently there is no reply. Therefore the Lord calls His own people to testify that He alone is God:

> I, even I, am the Lord
>   and beside me there is no saviour (vs. 8–14).

The form which His salvation is to take will be, first of all, the deliverance of Israel from captivity. This will be accomplished by the overthrow of Babylon, the proud city, which here is mentioned for the first time in this section of prophecy (vs. 14, 15).

The journey to Jerusalem will be more marvelous than the Exodus from Egypt. A "way" will be prepared for His people by the Lord according to His promise:

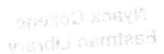

> I will give water in the wilderness
> > and rivers in the desert,
> to give drink to my people, my chosen (vs. 16–21).

Deliverance is not due to any desert on the part of Israel. They have failed to bring their offerings in the worship of God; rather they have "burdened" Him with their "sins" and "wearied" Him with their "iniquities." Yet pardon must precede deliverance. Only a penitent and forgiven people can enter upon the service of the Lord.

Therefore, pardon must be a matter of pure grace. Salvation is a free gift. In the Old Testament, as in the New, forgiveness comes from the unmerited favor of God:

> *I, even I, am he that blotteth out thy transgressions for mine own sake,*
> *and will not remember thy sins* (vs. 22–25).

Israel is challenged to prove any merit or to establish her innocence. The whole history has been one of failure and fault:

> Your first father [Jacob] sinned
> > and your teachers transgressed against me.
> Therefore I profaned the princes of the sanctuary,
> > I delivered Jacob to utter destruction
> and Israel to reviling (vs. 26–28).

On His people, thus forgiven and pardoned, God will pour out His Spirit. This will result in moral revival and national growth. It will be like the pouring out of "water on the thirsty land," and "streams on the dry ground." Only God can give such renewal, and He is the only God, beside Him there is no god (Ch. 44:1–8).

In striking contrast stand the impotent, lifeless, helpless gods which are made and worshiped by idolators. The prophet proceeds, with most unsparing irony, to ridicule the manufacture of these false deities. Nothing could be more absurd than to select a piece of wood, to use part of it to cook one's food and to fashion the rest of it into an image to be worshiped as a god. Probably the worshiper does not believe that he was made by that which he has made, but the prophet does indicate the absolute stupidity of idolatry. One who worships such a material, manufactured god, must be lacking in intelligence and reason. He has neither "knowledge" nor understanding; he "feeds on ashes," "a deluded mind has led him astray."

Yet how universal is idolatry! Men who do not all fall down in worship before images of wood or metal, do put other things in place of Deity as the supreme objects of their devotion. In its essence idolatry is a false idea of God. Even the early Christians, who had experienced a new birth and knew something of divine fellowship, needed to be warned by the Beloved Disciple: "Little children, keep yourselves from idols" (vs. 9–20) (I Jn. 5:21).

The prophet reminds Israel that it is God who has brought the nation into being, who has blotted out their sins as a vanishing cloud, and who bids them return to Him, their "Redeemer." The whole universe is called to unite in a hymn of praise for His saving work (vs. 21–23).

The agent in this redemption of Israel will be Cyrus. In an earlier chapter (Ch. 41:1–4, 25) reference has been made to this Persian king; now he is specifically named. The Lord who created heaven and earth, and who brought Israel into being, is able to foretell the work of this deliverer. The predictions of the Babylonian astrologers and diviners are "frustrated," or shown to be false; but God confirms the messages of His servants. It is He

> who saith to Jerusalem, Thou shalt be inhabited;
> and to the cities of Judah, ye shall be built, . . .
> that saith of Cyrus, He is my shepherd,
> and shall perform all my pleasure;
> even saying to Jerusalem, Thou shalt be built;
> and to the temple, Thy foundation shall be laid.

All this was fulfilled literally when, in 536 B.C., by the decree of Cyrus, the seventy years of captivity were ended and the restoration of Jerusalem was begun (vs. 24–28).

To this divinely appointed deliverer reference is made in the most remarkable terms. Not only is he the Lord's "shepherd" (Ch. 44:28) but also the Lord's "anointed," or "Messiah," "the man of my counsel," whom "I have called by my name," whom "the Lord loveth."

Undoubtedly he was a man of high character, represented by historians as a hero, a model of strength, of simplicity, of generosity, of wisdom and self-control. Yet it has been noted that Isaiah makes no mention of his moral qualities, but is concerned wholly with his military power and political influence.

He was an instrument in the hands of the Lord to whom all his strength was ascribed.

> Thus saith the Lord to his anointed, to Cyrus,
>   whose right hand I have grasped,
> to subdue nations before him
>   and ungird the loins of kings,
> to open doors before him
>   that gates may not be closed:
> I will go before you
>   and level the mountains,
> I will break in pieces the doors of bronze
>   and cut asunder the bars of iron,
> I will give you the treasures of darkness.

These conquests are not to glorify Cyrus, but to make the Lord know, from the farthest east to the farthest west, "that there is none beside me, I am the Lord, and there is none else."

The deliverance of Israel wrought by Cyrus will be a single event in the sovereign providence of God, with which conquests and calamities, as well as peace and prosperity, are concerned. The ultimate purpose of God is the salvation of His people. They well may join in the prayer:

> Drop down, ye heavens, from above,
>   and let the skies pour down righteousness;
> let the earth open, and let them bring forth salva-
>   tion,
>   and let righteousness spring up together (Ch.
>   45:1–8).

Some pious Israelites might be disturbed that a pagan conqueror should be predicted as the deliverer of God's people. The reply is severe and ironical. The course of Cyrus is wholly within the universal plan of God, and his decree to rebuild Jerusalem is but an incident in his long political career. Who are they that call into question the providences of God? They are themselves molded and controlled by divine power.

> Woe unto him that striveth with his Maker! . . .
> Shall the clay say to him that fashioneth it, What makest thou? . . .
> I have made the earth, and created man upon it;
> I, even my hands, have stretched out the heavens, and all their host have I commanded.
> I have raised him [Cyrus] up in righteousness, and I will direct all his ways:
> he shall build my city,
> and he shall let go my captives,
> not for price nor reward,
> saith the Lord of hosts (Ch. 45:9–13).

The vision of returning exiles and a city rebuilt inspires the prophet to predict a time when all nations will renounce their idols and turn to God as to the only Lord and Saviour.

> They shall be ashamed, and also confounded, all of them. . . .
> But Israel shall be saved in the Lord with an everlasting salvation.

Nor is it to Israel alone that the promise of redemption is made. The Lord who made the heavens and the earth, and who has the power to predict future events, sends forth His gracious invitation:

> *Look unto me, and be ye saved,*
> *all the ends of the earth.*

He promises a marvelous response:

> I have sworn by myself . . .
>   that unto me every knee shall bow,
>   every tongue shall swear (Ch. 45:14–25).

Isaiah 46

Is religion a burden or a blessing, is it a weight or wings, is it something you feel compelled to carry, or does it carry you? These questions which Isaiah raised in the minds of the ancient Hebrews were pertinent to the Jews in the days of our Lord, and are vital to the followers of Christ today.

The prophet was endeavoring to deliver Israel from the allurements of idolatry. He resorted to ridicule. He intimated the absurdity of worshiping gods which were absolutely helpless and must be carried about by the hands of men. He pictures an imaginary scene when Babylon is captured and idol images are being carried away to a place of safety, or seized as booty by the victor. The helpless gods are falling from their pedestals, and are being bound in bundles to be borne away as mere baggage on the backs of beasts:

> Bel boweth down, Nebo stoopeth,
>   their idols are on beasts and cattle;
> these things you carry are loaded
>   as burdens on weary beasts. . . .
> They themselves go into captivity (Ch. 46:1, 2).

In arresting contrast is the voice of the Lord:

> Even to your old age, I am he;
>   and even to hoar hairs will I carry you:
> I have made, and I will bear;
>   even I will carry, and will deliver you (vs. 4).

With scathing sarcasm the prophet depicts the idol: the work of a goldsmith, molded from metal, dragged through the streets to its silent shrine.

> Then they fall down and worship!
>   They lift it up upon their shoulders,
>   they carry it,
>   they set it in its place, and it stands there;
>   it cannot move from its place.
>   If one cries to it, it does not answer
>   or save him from his trouble.

How utterly different is the one eternal God, the All-wise, the All-powerful, who predicts the end from the beginning and brings to pass all that he predicts. He calls the conquering Cyrus "like a bird of prey from the east" to be the promised deliverer of Israel.

> I have spoken it, and I also will bring it to pass;
> I have purposed, I will also do it (v. 11).

With such striking contrasts, continually presented to their minds by the prophets, it is not strange that the Hebrew captives in Babylon practically abandoned the worship of idols.

Centuries passed, and when our Saviour appeared His people were worshiping the one living and true God, and yet their religion was a burden. It consisted in a wearisome round of rites, and ceremonies, of fasts and forms. They knew little of divine fellow-ship and redeeming grace. Then the Master sounded forth His gracious invitation:

> *Come unto me, all ye that labor and are*
> *heavy laden, and I will give you rest* (Matt.
> 11:28).

Why could He give them rest for their souls? He had just made the significant claim: "No man knoweth the Father but the Son, and he to whomsoever the Son will reveal him." Christ alone can give rest to the soul, since He alone can bring us to the Father. By communion with Him, in a life of obedience and faith and love, religion will be for us, not a system of cere-monies or of burdensome forms, but an experience of joy and exultation, of aspiration and of hope, through Jesus Christ our Lord.

Isaiah 47

In the minds of the inspired writers, Babylon was not only a city but also a symbol. It was, indeed, the imposing metropolis which stood on the banks of the Euphrates, and was known as the capital of a vast em-pire. To it the Hebrew captives were brought when Jerusalem had fallen, and there, for seventy years, they remained as exiles. However, the city was also a symbol of all the systems of false religion and heart-less political power which have sought to dominate the world. Its spirit was embodied long ago in the in-solent builders of the Tower of Babel, and was repro-duced in the cruel rulers of Rome pictured in the Apocalypse of John.

The prophet who predicted the deliverance of the Jews must first foretell the fall of Babylon. This he does in a mournful and significant dirge, which begins:

Come down and sit in the dust,
    O virgin daughter of Babylon;
sit on the ground without a throne,
    O daughter of the Chaldeans!

Thus the prophet personifies the city as a voluptuous conquered queen who is bidden to lay aside her royal robes and to grind with the millstones as a despised and naked slave. The One who decrees such degradation is none other than the Lord Himself, whom the prophet identifies by His unique titles:

I will take vengeance,
    and I will spare no man.
Our Redeemer—the Lord of hosts
    is his name—
the Holy One of Israel (Ch. 47:1–4).

The haughty princess, no longer "the mistress of kingdoms" will sit in darkness, in terror, and in silent despair. The Lord has meted out such suffering as a penalty for the heartless cruelty of the city. She has been chosen as the agent for chastisement of Israel, but she has overplayed her part. No mercy has been shown to the enslaved captives, not even to the most aged. This conduct was due to a self-confidence which was utterly disregardful of future calamity or retribution.

In her impious arrogance the city is supposed to make a claim which is proper for God alone:

I am, and there is no one besides me.

She boasts that no bereavement or loss could ever overtake her; she "felt secure" in her "wickedness"; but "in a moment, in one day, the loss of children and widowhood" would "come upon her in full measure," and this "in spite of her many sorceries and the great power" of her "enchantments."

The reputed wisdom of Babylon, which consisted largely in these enchantments and divinations, had betrayed the city into a false sense of security but could not deliver her from the "disaster" which suddenly was to fall (vs. 5–11).

In bitter irony she is challenged to depend upon her false counselors, whose incantations and charms have proved only wearisome and futile:

Perhaps you may be able to succeed; . . .
    let them stand up and save you, . . .

these astrologers and stargazers, and those who at the new moons predict future events, but are impotent and helpless. As stubble before the raging fire, they will be consumed. This will be no comforting, cheering fire, at which to warm oneself, but a fierce and destructive conflagration.

In the hour of disaster the city is deserted by those who selfishly have been enriched by her commerce. The merchants escape, "each in his own direction." Desolation and destruction are complete: "there is no one to save" (vs. 12–15).

Babylon must be overcome before Israel could be delivered, so the world power, which embodies her godless, cruel spirit, must be destroyed before the kingdom of Christ can fill the earth with its glory.

This chapter (48) is, in large measure, a summary of the eight chapters which precede; together they form a distinct section of this great prophecy (Chs. 40–48). The section concerns the deliverance of Judah from the captivity in Babylon; the chapter emphasizes the grace of God, His unique power to predict future events, His call of Cyrus to be the deliverer of the people, their past sufferings as deserved and as a divine discipline, and the certainty of their salvation and restoration.

The message is addressed to the exiles themselves. Their worship is formal and unreal, yet it expresses a faith and a religious inheritance to which an appeal can be made:

> Hear this, O house of Jacob,
>   who are called by the name of Israel,
> and who came forth from the loins of Judah,
>   who swear by the name of the Lord,
>   and confess the God of Israel,
>   but not in truth or right.

This imperfect faith should be strengthened by the remembrance of the divine predictions which had been fulfilled. God had foretold the events which He afterwards brought to pass, lest the rebellious people might ascribe them to the power of their false deities: "Lest you should say, 'My idol did them.'" (vs. 1–5). Thus God is now predicting "new things," namely, the deliverance from Babylon and the glorious restoration, so that the people could not claim to have expected these "new things": "Lest you should say, 'Behold, I knew them' " (vs. 6, 7). The disasters which have befallen Israel were in the nature of a divine discipline. God has not allowed the nation to be utterly destroyed. Such destruction would have reflected on His divine honor.

> For my name's sake I defer my anger,
>> for the sake of my praise I restrain it for you,
>> that I may not cut you off.
> Behold, I have refined you, but not like silver;
>> I have tried you in the furnace of affliction.
> For my own sake, for my own sake, I do it,
>> for how should my name be profaned? (vs.
>> 8–11).

Now the testing and the discipline are over. Deliverance is just at hand. The people can believe that God has power to keep His promise, for He is the Creator of all things:

> I am he, I am the first,
>> and I am the last.
> My hand laid the foundation of the earth,
>> and my right hand spread out the heavens
>> (vs. 12, 13).

As the agent of the coming deliverance, Cyrus has been divinely appointed.

> He shall perform his purpose on Babylon,
>> and his arm shall be against the Chaldeans.
> I, even I, have spoken and called him,
>> I have brought him, and he will prosper in his
>> way (vs. 14, 15).

The Lord loves His people. He is ever their Redeemer and their Guide. Their sufferings have been due to their disobedience. They were not necessary:

> O that you had hearkened to my commandments!
>   Then your peace would have been like a river,
> And your righteousness like the waves of the sea,
>   your offspring would have been like the
>   sand, . . .
> their name would never be cut off (vs. 16–19).

At last the hour of deliverance has come, and the command is spoken to leave the scenes of their exile:

> Go forth from Babylon, flee from Chaldea,
>   declare this with a shout of joy, proclaim it,
> send it forth to the end of the earth;
>   say, The Lord has redeemed his servant
>   Jacob (v. 20).

This deliverance is to be as marvelous as the Exodus from Egypt and its mercies as great as those of the wilderness journey:

> They thirsted not when he led them
>   through the deserts;
> he made water flow for them from the rock;
>   he cleft the rock and the water gushed out
>   (v. 21).

This promise of deliverance was likewise a command. The exiles were to go forth to the ends of the earth as witnesses of God's redemption.

Thus today those who know the salvation of the Lord are to trust in His protecting care on their wilderness way, and are to bear to all the world the message of redeeming love.

The marvelous promise, however, is limited; not all are to expect deliverance and blessedness.

> "There is no peace," saith the Lord,
>   to the wicked" (v. 22).

With these solemn words this section of the great prophecy (Chs. 40–48) comes to its close.

2. THE SERVANT OF THE LORD [CHS. 49–57]

The preceding chapters have predicted the deliverance of Israel from the captivity in Babylon; the agent is to be Cyrus. In this section the horizon is widened; redemption is promised for the whole world. The Deliverer is to be no military chieftain, but a spiritual Redeemer, who is called "The Servant of the Lord."

This unique and enigmatic Figure has appeared before and is the most prominent Person in this portion of the Prophecy (Chs. 40–66). Four paragraphs in particular define His character and mission. These are known as the *"Servant-Songs"* (Ch. 42:1–9; 49:1–13; 50:4–9; 52:13–53:12).

A review of these prophetic poems leads to the conclusion that the "Servant" is a personification of Israel, but in three distinct aspects. First, the phrase represents the nation as a whole, the people chosen of God and commissioned to be His messenger to all the world. Second, the words indicate the godly portion of the people, the "Israel within Israel," the righteous remnant, the pious core or kernel, which recognizes

its privileges, its duty, and its destiny, and seeks to
bring the rebellious mass of the people back to their
God so that they may witness for Him among the nations. Third, the "Servant" is not only a personification but a Person. He embodies in Himself all the
noblest qualities and ideals of His people, and through
vicarious suffering becomes the Saviour of the world.
Their can be no doubt that the prediction of such a
Saviour is fulfilled only in the person and work of our
Lord Jesus Christ.

The *first* of these four *"Songs"* (Ch. 42:1–9) celebrated the gentle and gracious character of the "Servant," His courage, His divine support, and His world-
wide mission, all of which was applied by Matthew
specifically to the earthly ministry of our Lord (Matt.
12:18–21).

In the *second* *"Song"* the "Servant" speaks for
Himself. He addresses the inhabitants of the farthest
lands, as commissioned in the previous poem (Ch.
42:4). He claims a divine call to His prophetic task;
His preparation was "like a sharp sword" in the scab-
bard of the Lord, or a "polished arrow in his quiver":
and through His ministry the Lord is to be glorified
(Ch. 49:1–3).

Although His service seems fruitless at first, and
He fails to bring His people into fellowship with God,
He is divinely encouraged by the assurance of the future return of Israel and of His own mission to the
whole world:

I will also give you as a light to the nations,
  that my salvation may reach to the end of the
  earth (vs. 4–6).

To Israel there is promised a marvelous reversal of fortune. The nation which has been "despised" and "abhorred" shall be honored and worshiped by "kings" and "princes." There is to be "an acceptable time" (a "time of favor"), a "day of salvation," and the exiles are to be set free. They are pictured as sheep of which the Lord is their Shepherd.

> They shall feed along the ways,
>   on all bare heights shall be their pasture;
> they shall not hunger or thirst,
>   neither scorching wind nor sun shall smite
>   them,
> for he who has pity on them will lead them,
>   and by springs of water will guide them
>   (vs. 7–12).

Thus we hear in advance the strains of heavenly music which John, centuries later, applied to the hosts of the redeemed:

> They shall hunger no more, neither thirst any more; neither shall the sun light on them, nor any heat. For the Lamb which is in the midst of the throne shall feed them, and shall lead them unto living fountains of water; and God shall wipe away all tears from their eyes (Rev. 7:16, 17).

As Isaiah beholds the returning exiles, it is no wonder that he raises a hymn of praise:

> Sing for joy, O heavens, and exult, O earth;
>   break forth, O mountains, into singing!
> For the Lord has comforted his people,
>   and will have compassion on his afflicted
>   (vs. 12, 13).

However, in the face of such promises doubts arise. The people need to be reassured:

> But Zion said, The Lord has forsaken me,
>   my Lord has forgotten me.

The Lord replies that though a mother might forget her helpless child,

> Yet I will not forget you.
>   Behold, I have graven you on the palms of my
>   hands;
> your walls are ever before me (vs. 14–16).

Zion is to be rebuilt, and the city will be overtaxed by its population (vs. 18–21). The Lord will lift up His hand as a signal and the Gentile nations will conduct home the scattered exiles of Judah. Kings and queens will supply their needs and render homage (vs. 22, 23).

There is another question which feeble faith may ask: Not only does God remember, but is He able to deliver His people? The answer is in the form of a striking poetic inversion:

> Can the prey be taken from the mighty,
>   or the captives of a tyrant be rescued?
> Surely, thus says the Lord:
>   Even the captives of the mighty shall be taken,
>   and the prey of the tyrant be rescued,
>   for I will contend with those who contend with
>   you,
>   and I will save your children.

The enemies of Israel shall be divided in bitter strife and shall destroy one another. "Then all flesh shall know that I am the Lord your Saviour, and your Redeemer, the Mighty One of Jacob (vs. 24–26).

To further encourage the captives they are assured that their servitude is not permanent. They are addressed as children of Zion. It must not be supposed that the Lord has formally divorced their mother, nor that they have been sold to some creditors. Zion, indeed, has been unfaithful, but no final bill of divorcement has been given her; and as for creditors, to whom could the Lord be in debt? Their exile has been due to their own sins:

> Behold, for your iniquities you were sold,
>   and for your transgressions your mother
>   was put away (Ch. 50:1).

If only Israel will repent and will trust in God, pardon is possible and deliverance assured. The Lord who controls all the powers of nature doubtless can redeem His people. Yet all His messages of grace and mercy have been unheeded:

> Wherefore when I came, was there no man?
>   when I called, was there none to answer
>   (vs. 2, 3).

The reference to messages and messengers somewhat lessens the abruptness with which the *third* of the *"Servant Songs"* is introduced (Ch. 50:4–9). Again the Servant is speaking, although He is not specifically named. Now He is addressing neither the nations nor His own people. His utterance is in the form of a soliloquy. He is realizing the dignity and importance of His prophetic office, but also its peril. He listens daily for the divine message and thus is enabled to give courage to those who are faint:

> The Lord hath given me the tongue of the
>   learned,
>   that I should know how to speak a word in
>   season
>   to him that is weary:
> he waketh morning by morning, he waketh mine
>   ear to hear as the learned.
> The Lord God hath opened mine ear,
>   and I was not rebellious,
> neither turned away back (vs. 4, 5).

He knew well enough the fate which men usually mete out to the true prophets; they are scorned and scourged, are sawn asunder, are burned, beheaded, stoned and crucified. Yet he was undismayed:

> I gave my back to the smiters,
>   and my cheek to them that plucked off the hair;
> I hid not my face from shame and spitting (v. 6).

His courage does not fail:

> For the Lord God will help me;
>   therefore I shall not be confounded;
>   therefore have I set my face like a flint,
> and I know that I shall not be ashamed (v. 7).

His enemies will be consumed, and he will be vindicated against those who may claim that his sufferings were deserved:

> He is near that justified me;
>   who will contend with me?

> Let us stand together:
>   who is mine adversary?
>   Let him come near to me.
> Behold, the Lord God will help me;
>   who is he that shall condemn me? (vs. 8, 9)

The prophet himself now addresses the godly portion of the people. In "darkness" and distress they are to depend on the Lord as the "Servant" has done:

> Who is among you that feareth the Lord,
>   that obeyeth the voice of his servant,
>   that walketh in darkness
>   and hath no light?
> Let him trust in the name of the Lord,
>   and stay upon his God (v. 10).

On the other hand, those who refused to hear the voice of the prophet, and sought to kindle fires of their own, would be doomed to "lie down in sorrow," in disillusion and anguish. Again and again such solemn warnings conclude paragraphs of radiant prediction. Not all Israel are the true Israel and heirs of the promises (v. 11).

Now the Lord, not the prophet, is heard to speak and to encourage the exiles to expect a speedy return (Ch. 51:1 to 52:12). The section opens with three brief paragraphs, each of which begins with the phrase: "Harken unto me" (vs. 1, 4, 7). The address is to the righteous, who attend to the word of the Lord. They are to remember the past mercies of God, and therefore to have no present fear. He made a great nation to spring from Abraham, who long had been childless; He is surely able to restore Zion and to make her pres-

ent desolation like Eden, and cause her to be filled
with joy and "gladness" and "the voice of melody"
(Ch. 51:1–3).

The "law of the Lord" and a true knowledge of
Him will be for a "light to the Gentiles." His salvation shall go forth to the most distant peoples. He can
be trusted, for He has created the heavens and the
earth and is to continue forever (vs. 4–6). Those who
serve the Lord need have no fear. Their enemies are
soon to perish, but the faithfulness of the Lord "shall
be forever" and His salvation from generation to generation" (vs. 7, 8).

Three other passages follow, each one of which
again begins with an identical phrase, *"Awake, awake"*
(Ch. 51:9, 51:17; 52:1). The appeal is addressed to
the Lord. Let Him now act as He acted when His
people were led forth from Egypt; then the exiles will
be led forth from Babylon in triumph:

> *The redeemed of the Lord shall return,*
> *and come with singing unto Zion;*
> *and everlasting joy shall be upon their head:*
> *they shall obtain gladness and joy;*
> *and sorrow and mourning shall flee away.*

To this appeal the Lord makes reply:

> I, even I, am he that comforts you.

If you fear frail mortal man it must be because
you have forgotten me your Maker, who has "stretched
out the heavens, and laid the foundations of the
earth." You need not dread the "fury of the oppressor." The captive "shall speedily be released," "for

I am the Lord thy God, who stirs up the waves of the sea." "I have put my word in your mouth, saying to Zion, Thou art my people" (vs. 9–16).

The second call to *"awake"* is even more forcible, and implies that Zion can arouse herself from the stupor only by a supreme effort. She has been made to drink the "cup of wrath" and the "bowl of staggering." She is helpless and hopeless. None of her sons has stretched out a hand to relieve her; they likewise have suffered, and lie as dead men in the open places of the city.

Yet she has suffered enough. The cup of anguish will be taken from her hand and placed in the hand of those who have tormented her and have said to her "Bow down, that we may pass over," and have treated with scorn her prostrate body (vs. 17–23).

The third call to *"awake"* introduces a sudden contrast:

> Awake, awake, put on thy strength, O Zion;
>   put on thy beautiful garments,
> O Jerusalem, the holy city.

The "daughter of Zion" who has been prostrate in the dust, degraded, debased, is to assume her royal, festal robes, to be enthroned and to await the return of her King (Ch. 52:1, 2). Her captors paid nothing for her, they can claim nothing for her release. Egypt and Assyria oppressed her without cause, but she was delivered, as now she shall be set free from Babylon. Her sufferings at the hands of idolaters have caused the name of the Lord to be blasphemed, but He is now to be vindicated and His name to be reverenced as of

the One who has intervened and brought deliverance
(vs. 3–6).

Now the promise is fulfilled; Babylon has fallen;
the people are free; a herald is approaching Zion to
announce that the King is on His way, and will soon
appear.

> *How beautiful upon the mountains*
>   *are the feet of him that bringeth good tidings,*
> *that publisheth peace; that bringeth good tidings*
>   *of good,*
>   *that publisheth salvation;*
> *that saith unto Zion, Thy God reigneth* (v. 7).

The watchmen on the dismantled walls take up the
cry:

> Hark, your watchmen lift up their voice,
>   together they sing for joy;
>   for eye to eye they see
> the return of the Lord to Zion (v. 8).

Even the ruins of Jerusalem are to celebrate the great
deliverance which is to be witnessed by the uttermost
parts of the earth:

> Break forth together into singing,
>   you waste places of Jerusalem;
> for the Lord has comforted his people,
>   he has redeemed Jerusalem.
> The Lord has laid bare his holy arm
>   before the eyes of all the nations;
> *and all the ends of the earth shall see*
>   *the salvation of our God* (vs. 9, 10).

The exiles are summoned to leave Babylon, but they must be pure and consecrated to the Lord, as they were to carry back to Jerusalem the sacred vessels which had been taken from the temple; and as they were to be accompanied by God Himself they were not to "go out in haste" and fear, as when they left Egypt; but as God led them on the wilderness journey by a pillar of cloud, so now He would be both their vanguard and their rearguard, their Defender as well as their Guide (vs. 11, 12).

The *fourth* of the *"Servant Songs"* (Ch. 52:13–53:12) contains what is probably the best known and most precious chapter of all the prophecies of Isaiah (Ch. 53). Its music must not be broken by extended comments, but some of its notes properly may be prolonged. The main purpose of every reader should be to find how perfectly this portrayal of *The Suffering Servant* is fulfilled by our *Lord Jesus Christ*.

It should be noted that the poem consists of five paragraphs or strophes, each containing three verses. The first of these strophes concludes Chapter 52, and is an essential part of the "Song" (Ch. 52:13–15). It describes the future *exaltation* of the *"Servant"* following His deep humilation; and it reveals the truth that suffering may be part of a mysterious divine plan and may issue in triumph and glory:

> Behold, my servant shall deal prudently [or shall prosper],
>> he shall be exalted and extolled, and be very high.
> As many were astonished at him (or thee)—

> His appearance was so marred, beyond human
>> resemblance,
>> and his form beyond that of the sons of men—
> so shall he startle [or sprinkle] many nations;
> kings shall shut their mouths at him [in dumb
>> adoration];
>> for that which had not been told them they
>> shall see,
> and that which they have not heard,
>> they shall consider [or understand].

The next strophe (Ch. 53:1–3) depicts the "servant" as *misunderstood, despised,* and *rejected.* His circumstances and His appearance inspired neither admiration nor respect. He lived in humility and obscurity and was familiar with sickness and poverty and pain, and therefore was not recognized as the divine messenger.

"Who hath believed our report?" That is, who has believed what has been reported to us, concerning this Saviour and Redeemer. The implied answer is, "No one."

"And to whom is the arm of the Lord revealed," who has really understood the divine purpose and plan?

> For he shall grow up before him as a tender plant,
>> and as a root out of a dry ground;
> he hath no form nor comeliness;
>> and when we shall see him,
> there is no beauty that we should desire him.
> He is despised and rejected of men;
>> a man of sorrows and acquainted with grief;

> and as one from whom men hide their faces
>> he was despised and we esteemed him not.

Men supposed that His sufferings were deserved and were due to divine displeasure. They were all endured for the sake of others. Nowhere in Scripture is the reality of *vicarious sufferings* more forcefully set forth than in this third strophe (vs. 4–9).

> Surely he hath borne our griefs,
>> and carried our sorrows;
> yet we did esteem him stricken,
>> smitten by God, and afflicted.
> But he was wounded for our transgressions,
>> he was bruised for our iniquities;
> the chastisement that made us whole was upon
>> him;
>> and with his stripes we are healed.
> All we like sheep have gone astray;
>> we have turned every one to his own way;
> and the Lord hath laid on him
>> the iniquity of us all.

The fourth strophe describes the *meekness* and the *ignominious death* of the "Servant" (vs. 7–9).

> He was oppressed, and he was afflicted,
>> yet he opened not his mouth;
> like a lamb that is led to the slaughter,
>> and like a sheep that before its shearers is
>> dumb.
> so he opened not his mouth.
> By oppression and judgment he was taken away.

(It was by violence cloaked under the formalities of a legal process.)

> And as for his generation, who considered
>> that he was cut off out of the land of the living,
>> stricken for the transgression of my people?
> And they made his grave with the wicked
>> and with a rich man in his death,
>> although he had done no violence,
>> and there was no deceit in his mouth.

The *vindication and reward* of the *"Suffering Servant"* are expressed in the fifth and last strophe of this matchless mournful triumphant poem (vs. 10–12). The sufferings and humiliation just related were due to no fault of the Servant, nor to accident, nor to blind fate. All were related to a divine purpose. He was innocent,

> Yet it was the will of the Lord to bruise him;
>> he has put him to grief.

The purpose is now made clear. It was in order that, by making Himself a "guilt-offering," atonement might be made and sins be forgiven. Or to state this purpose more fully:

> When he makes himself an offering for sin,
>> he shall see his offspring, he shall prolong his
>>> days;
> the will of the Lord shall prosper in his hand.

That is, as a result of all His suffering, a new-born family will appear, and endless life will issue and the purpose of the Lord will be accomplished.

Furthermore, He will bring many into a right relation with God. He will "justify many," or "make them to be accounted righteous."

> He shall see of the travail of his soul and be satisfied;
>> by his knowledge shall the righteous one, my servant,
> make many to be accounted righteous;
>> and he shall bear their iniquities.

The supreme exaltation which is promised will be due to His sacrificial death and to His "intercession" or His "intervention" in behalf of many:

> Therefore will I divide him a portion with the great,
>> and he shall divide the spoil with the strong;
> because he poured out his soul to death,
>> and was numbered with the transgressors;
> yet he bore the sin of many,
>> and made intercession for the transgressors.

One who ponders reverently and thoughtfully this marvelous Song of the Suffering Servant cannot fail to perceive how perfectly it predicted the voluntary, sacrificial, vicarious death of Christ. To its haunting strains the believing heart replies in the words of the apostle,

> He died for all, that those who live might live no longer for themselves, but for him who for their sake died and rose again (II Cor. 5:15).

A part of the reward promised to the "Suffering Servant" (Ch. 53) was to consist in His "seed," or His multiplied descendants, and in the "many" who would share in His redeeming work. This same truth is now expanded as the prophet depicts the increased numbers of Zion's children which will dwell in Jerusalem after the return from exile. He employs figures of speech to which the counterpart can be found in New Testament symbolism. John, in the Apocalypse, described the glorified church as a bride and also as a city.

So Isaiah encourages the Jewish exiles by comparing their nation to a wife who belongs to the Lord as her Husband, and then to a city of jewels and gems. These two comparisons constitute the substance of

Chapter 54.

> Sing, O barren one, who did not bear,
>   break forth into singing and cry aloud. . . .
> For the children of the desolate
>   one will be more
> than the children of her that is married,
>   says the Lord (v. 1).

Zion, personified during the captivity as a childless wife, should rejoice as she is to become the mother of more children than before the exile. She will need to increase the size of her dwelling. Therefore the command comes:

> Enlarge the place of your tent, . . . lengthen
>   your cords
>   and strengthen your stakes (v. 2).
> For you will spread abroad to the
>   right and to the left,

and your descendants will possess the nations
    and will people the desolate cities (v. 3).

Judah will forget the shame of her youth, when she
was idolatrous and disobedient, and the reproach of
her widowhood when she was a captive in Babylon.

For your Maker is your husband,
    the Lord of hosts is his name. . . .
For a brief moment I forsook you,
    but with great compassion I will gather
    you. . . .
With everlasting love I will have compassion on
    you,
    says the Lord, your Redeemer. . . .
For the mountains may depart
    and the hills be removed,
but my steadfast love shall not depart from you
    (vs. 4–10).

Now the figure of speech changes, and the description of the future glory of Judah reminds one not only
of the "Bride of the Lamb" but of the "Holy City,"
the "New Jerusalem." John pictures the "walls of
jasper, the foundations of precious stones, the gates of
pearl, and the street of gold" (Rev. 21:18–21). So
Isaiah describes "foundations of sapphires, pinnacles
of agate, gates of carbuncles, and a wall of precious
stones" (vs. 11, 12).

Yet prosperity and security are not assured by
numbers or wealth. Moral character alone can be the
hope of a nation. So the children of Judah are to be
"taught by the Lord," and "in righteousness you shall
be established" (vs. 13, 14).

The city is to be not only glorious but safe, and free from oppression and fear and terror. If enemies "gather together" against the people of God it will not be by divine command and therefore they shall fail. God has created men who have made and cruelly used weapons of war, but the promise here is this:

No weapon formed against thee shall prosper,

and every false accusation shall be defeated and re-pelled. Such security is the lawful possession and the right of Zion:

> This is the heritage of the servants of the Lord
> and their vindication from me,
> says the Lord (vs. 13–17).

Chapter 55.

> Ho, every one that thirsteth,
> come ye to the waters;
> and he that hath no money,
> come ye, buy and eat;
> yea, come, buy wine and milk
> without money and without price.
> Wherefore do ye spend money for
> that which is not bread?
> and your labor for that which satisfieth not?
> Hearken diligently unto me,
> and eat ye that which is good,
> and let your soul delight itself in fatness (Ch.
> 55:1–2).

This *gracious invitation* was addressed to the Jewish exiles. They were homesick. Weary of the hot, dusty plains of Babylon, they longed for the hills and streams and fields of Canaan; they "wept when they remembered Zion." More pitiful still, they were heart-sick. They were attempting to live without God. By daily toil or the eager pursuit of wealth and pleasure they were striving to satisfy their souls, but they were spiritually faint and hungry and thirsty. They were spending their money for that which was not (really) "bread." Such coin is not current in the realm of the spirit.

Then came the divine call: "Hearken diligently unto me." When there is obedience to God and trust in Him, there will be not only water for the thirsty but "wine and milk." The soul will "delight itself in fatness," that is, in a rich supply of spiritual food. All this will be given in pure grace; it may be purchased "without money and without price." Yet those who would receive must "come," they must "hearken," they must obey.

> Incline your ear, and come unto me;
> > hear, and your soul shall live;
> and I will make an everlasting covenant with you,
> > even the sure mercies of David.
> Behold, I have given him for a witness to the people,
> > a leader and commander to the people.
> Behold, thou shalt call a nation
> > that thou knowest not,
> and nations that knew not thee
> > shall run unto thee,

because of the Lord thy God,
   and for the Holy One of Israel;
for he hath glorified thee (vs. 3–5).

Thus, to those who would hear and obey there was the assurance of new spiritual life and of all the blessings promised to David. These would include, and find as their climax, the Person and work of the Son of David who has been represented as the "Suffering Servant" (Chapter 53), but who was to be, by virtue of His vicarious death, a divine "Witness" to the truth, the "Captain" of salvation, the "King of kings." Thus a repentant and obedient Israel would be a channel of blessing to all the nations of the world.

However, immediate action is necessary; delay may be fatal. Therefore the prophet issues the vital command:

Seek ye the Lord while he may be found,
   call ye upon him while he is near;
let the wicked forsake his way,
   and the unrighteous man his thoughts:
and let him return unto the Lord; and
   he will have mercy upon him;
and to our God, for he will abundantly pardon
   (vs. 6, 7).

The way of salvation could hardly be stated more clearly. Whether for the nation or for each individual, there must be a complete reversal of the "way" of life resulting from a change of thought and purpose. Those who do "return unto the Lord" can be certain to receive His gracious forgiveness, His abundant pardon. Such a change is necessary, and one is encouraged to seek the Lord in view of the contrast between the "ways" and the "thoughts" of God and man:

> For my thoughts are not your thoughts,
>> neither are your ways my ways,
>> saith the Lord.
> For as the heavens are higher than the earth,
>> so are my ways higher than your ways,
> and my thoughts than your thoughts (vs. 8, 9).

The mention of the heavens implies the rich provision which the Lord makes for those who receive and obey His word:

> For as the rain cometh down,
>> and the snow from heaven,
> and returneth not thither,
>> but watereth the earth and
> maketh it bring forth and bud,
>> that it may give seed to the sower
> and bread to the eater:
>> so shall my word be
> that goeth forth out of my mouth:
>> it shall not return unto me void,
> but it shall accomplish that which I please
>> and it shall prosper in the thing whereto I sent
>>> it (vs. 10, 11).

Last of all is the description of the glad new life of the people who return to the Lord. All nature seems to be changed before them. To the music of the mountains the waving branches of the trees applaud. Worthless shrubs are replaced by fir and myrtle symbolizing the new life of the spirit. The marvelous transformation will be an abiding memorial to the grace and power of God:

> For ye shall go out with joy,
>> and be led forth with peace;
> the mountains and the hills shall break forth
>> before you into singing,
> and all the trees of the field
>> shall clap their hands.
> Instead of the thorn shall come up the fir tree,
>> and instead of the brier shall come up the
>> myrtle tree:
> and it shall be to the Lord for a name,
>> for an everlasting sign that shall not be cut off
>> (vs. 12, 13).

Pardon is free. The fulness of life is the gift of God; it is "without money and without price." "By grace are ye saved through faith." However, "faith" must be so real and vital as to be manifest in "works." Those who enjoy fellowship with God must trust and obey.

Thus, to the "gracious invitation" (Chapter 55) extended to the returning exiles, the following exhortation is added:

> Thus says the Lord:
>> Keep ye justice and do righteousness;
> for soon my salvation will come,
>> and my deliverance be revealed.
> Blessed is the man who does this,
>> and the son of man who holds it fast,

> who keeps the sabbath, not profaning it,
>> and keeps his hand from doing any evil (Ch.
>> 56:1, 2).

Keeping the Sabbath was the accepted sign of loyalty
to God, and refraining from evil was a symbol of right
relations to man. To those whose faith was expressed
by such conduct there was promised the privilege of
worshiping with the people of God, and also all the
blessings this privilege might include. Even persons
of foreign birth, or those forbidden by the Jewish
ceremonial law, would be welcomed to the house of
the Lord:

> These I will bring to my holy mountain,
>> and make them joyful in my house of
>> prayer. . . .
> for my house shall be called a house of prayer
>> for all peoples.
> Thus says the Lord God,
>> who gathers the outcasts of Israel,
> I will gather yet others to him
>> besides those already gathered (vs. 3–8).

It was the Saviour of the whole world who quoted
these words in the temple at Jerusalem: "My house
shall be called a house of prayer for all the nations"
(Mark 11:17). He it was who brought the Glad
Tidings that, no matter what one is by birth, and re-
gardless of what laws may have been broken, "who-
soever will" may come and "take the water of life
freely" (Rev. 22:17).

In a startling transition from these gracious
promises the prophet turns to pronounce the punish-

ment of evil, even when it appears among the people of God. The enemies of Israel are summoned to do their work, which may be regarded as a divine discipline:

> All ye beasts of the field, come to devour,
>   yea, all ye beasts in the forest (v. 9).

The nation is thus pictured as a helpless flock endangered by fierce wolves. The leaders, who should have warned and protected the people, are compared to worthless watchdogs, blind, unable to bark, sleepy, hungry; or they are likened to shepherds, stupid, greedy, sensual, drunken. Under such rulers, righteous men die unnoticed and unlamented, and are fortunate to rest in their graves (Ch. 56:10–57:2).

Next, the prophet rebukes the faithless people for their besetting sins of idolatry and political intrigue. The worship of false gods was regarded as spiritual adultery; it was a breach of the covenant between God and His people. This idolatry had been practiced insolently, openly, in every grove and valley and on every high hill. It had been accompanied by foul orgies, and even by the offering of children as sacrifices.

In seeking foreign political alliances they had sent messengers to great distances and had debased themselves by offering rich bribes and accepting humiliating terms (Ch. 57:3–10).

For such sins judgment will surely fall. In fear of men, the people had forgotten God. He had shown such long forbearance that they had ceased to fear Him. Punishment is coming, and then all their "collection" of impotent, helpless idols will be swept away, as by a breath of wind. However, the righteous would be saved:

> He who takes refuge in me shall
> possess the land,
> and shall inherit my holy mountain (vs. 11–13).

For the return of the repentant remnant a highway will be prepared, and every barrier be removed:

> And it shall be said,
> Build up, build up, prepare the way,
> remove every obstruction from my people's way
> (v. 14).

The vital truth for the comfort of the faithful, lies in the nature of God himself; the infinitely Great cares for the infinitely small:

> For thus saith the high and lofty One
> that inhabiteth eternity, whose name is Holy:
> *I dwell in the high and holy place,*
> *with him also that is of a contrite and humble*
> *spirit,*
> *to revive the spirit of the humble,*
> *and to revive the heart of the contrite ones* (v. 15).

A further word of comfort is spoken to those who are still suffering for their sins: "I will not contend forever." The time of God's chastisement is limited; otherwise the souls He has created would be consumed, and His purpose in creation be frustrated. Stubborn disobedience had made necessary the punishment; but now God recognizes the repentance. He will heal and comfort, and give occasion for thanksgiving and praise (vs. 16–18).

The whole message of salvation is summed up in the universal promise of peace:

> *Peace, peace to him that is far off,*
>   *and to him that is near, saith the Lord;*
> *and I will heal him* (v. 19).

The promise, however, is not unconditional:

> But the wicked are like the troubled sea;
>   for it cannot rest,
> and its waters toss up mire and dirt.
> *There is no peace, saith my God,*
>   *to the wicked* (vs. 20, 21).

3. THE PERFECTED KINGDOM OF GOD [CHS. 58–66]

The climax of this marvelous book of prophecy is found in its closing chapters (58–66). Their chief feature is the impressive picture of Jerusalem, when the Jewish exiles shall have been restored to their own land. All nations will turn to the resplendent city, the crowning glory of which will be the holiness of its people.

However, the promises of God and the blessings of His salvation, are conditioned on faith and obedience. Therefore, the first two of these concluding chapters contain a call to repentance.

The task of the prophet is announced. He must speak with boldness, with severity, yet with compassion:

> Cry aloud, spare not, lift up your
>   voice like a trumpet;

> declare to my people their transgression,
>> to the house of Jacob their sins (Ch. 58:1).

Thus the message of Isaiah is that proclaimed later by John the Baptist: "Repent ye: for the kingdom of heaven is at hand" (Matt. 3:2).

The chief fault rebuked by the prophet is that of religious *formalism*. This seems to be the besetting sin of God's people. Nowhere else in Scripture is there a more keen and incisive analysis of this sin. The most pitiful phase is that which is here portrayed. The formalist does not know that he is a formalist. He is not a mere hypocrite; he is not an actor playing a part; but he is serious and scrupulous in performing all the ceremonies of his accepted ritual. Yet in his mind there is little thought of God, and in his heart no love for man. There results no satisfaction of soul, no peace, no divine fellowship.

These formalists complain that God is blind and indifferent to their worship:

> Why have we fasted, and thou seest it not?
> Why have we humbled ourselves,
>> and thou takest no knowledge of it?

The answer is immediate. Your worship is not true worship; your fasting is not real fasting. At the very time of your fast you are seeking your own pleasure; you are cruel to your servants; you are showing violence to your neighbors, and you misunderstand God. He is not pleased that, in refraining from food, you are making yourselves miserable. Self-denial without a worthy purpose is a travesty upon religion (vs. 3–5).

There is a real "fast" which does honor God. Self-sacrifice may be shown in delivering the enslaved, in feeding the hungry, in clothing and sheltering the poor. Let your worship be united with charity,

Then shall your light break forth
like the morning. . . .
You shall call, and the Lord will answer. . . .
The Lord will guide you continually. . . .
Your ancient ruins shall be rebuilt; . . .
you shall be called the repairer of the breach,
the restorer of paths to dwell in (vs. 6–12).

Formalism is sinful, yet the most spiritual religion must have its forms, and the service of men must not be regarded as a substitute for the worship of God. Thus, when the prophet has insisted that a true ritual will be united with charity, and will find its issue in divine fellowship, he now emphasizes the absolute need of one religious form, namely, the observance of the Sabbath. Through all the ages this has been regarded as the supreme sign and symbol of devotion to God and dedication to His service.

In these modern days it is well to emphasize anew these immortal words of Isaiah:

If you turn back your foot from the sabbath,
from doing your pleasure on my holy day,
and call the sabbath a delight
and the holy day of the Lord honorable;
if you honor it, not going your own ways,
or seeking your own pleasure, or talking idly;
then you shall take delight in the Lord,
and I will make you ride upon
the high places of the earth;

> I will feed you with the heritage of
>   Jacob your father,
> for the mouth of the Lord has spoken (vs. 13, 14).

What, then, has hidden the face of the Lord and retarded the deliverance He has promised? Surely it has been no lack of knowledge or power on His part, but solely the sins of His people:

> Behold, the Lord's hand is not shortened, that it
>   cannot save,
>   or his ear dull, that it cannot hear;
> but your iniquities have made a separation
>   between you and your God,
> and your sins have hid his face from you
>   so that he does not hear (Ch. 59:1, 2).

These sins the prophet proceeds to detail in all their blackness. The language is picturesque and figurative, but vividly clear in its lurid portrayal. The whole course of life is declared to be unclean; hands, feet, lips, tongue, all are defiled. In the courts of law there is no justice. The purposes of the people produce only malignant evil like the hatching of vipers' eggs, and their flimsy pleas are as the webs of spiders:

> Their feet run to evil,
>   and they make haste to shed innocent blood. . . .
> The way of peace they know not,
>   and there is no justice in their paths (vs. 3–8).

The prophet then identifies himself with his people in a paragraph of humble confession. He voices their helplessness, their degradation, their mournful distress.

Our transgressions are with us,
>   and we know our iniquities,
transgressing, and denying the Lord,
>   and turning away from following our God. . . .
Truth is lacking, and he who departs from evil
>   makes himself a prey (vs. 9–15).

"The Lord saw it." He saw the sin and the repentance and also the helplessness of the people. He was grieved "that there was no man" to intervene, to rescue, to save. Therefore, He arms Himself as a warrior, but His weapons are spiritual. He put on a breastplate of righteousness, "a helmet of salvation," "vengeance" as clothing, and "zeal" for a mantle.

According to their deed, so will he repay,
>   wrath to his adversaries, recompense to his
>   enemies.

As a result of his intervention the whole world will learn to "fear the name of the Lord."

Man may fulfill the conditions of salvation by repentance and faith, but only God can save.

He will come to Zion as Redeemer,
>   to those in Jacob who turn from transgression.

It is to the "believing remnant," to the true Zion, that the prophet is ever repeating his promises. With them the Redeemer will make a new covenant, one ministered by the Spirit and the Word, one that will continue forever and forever (vs. 15b–21).

All is now ready. Deliverance from captivity has been assured. A highway has been prepared for the return. A Redeemer has been promised. The conditions of salvation have been made plain. To complete the prophecy it remains only that Zion shall appear in her predicted glory. Therefore a voice is heard:

> *Arise, shine; for your light has come,*
>   *and the glory of the Lord has risen upon you*
>   (Ch. 60:1).

It is the light of the Divine Presence, the light of the promised Restoration, which has burst forth like a radiant dawn upon the restored city. Nor is it for the benefit of the city alone that the light shines; but its glory is to attract to it all the peoples of the world:

> For behold, darkness shall cover the earth,
>   and thick darkness the peoples;
> but the Lord will arise upon you,
>   and his glory will be seen upon you.
> And nations shall come to your light,
>   and kings to the brightness of your rising (vs. 2, 3).

They come aiding the returning exiles, and bearing treasures from all quarters of the earth. The prophet takes his stand on Mount Zion, and looking toward the east he sees the caravans streaming over the hills of Moab toward Jerusalem with their precious burdens. He looks toward the west, and over the Great Sea he envisions fleets of ships with their rich cargoes. The white sails look "like a cloud" driven by the wind, or "doves" winging to "their windows." The use of all these treasures is the enrichment of the house of the Lord and the glory of his name (vs. 4-9).

The walls of the city shall be rebuilt by "foreigners," whose kings shall be the servants of its people. The gates of the city "shall be open continually" to receive "the wealth of the nations." Hostile kingdoms shall perish. The precious trees of Lebanon will be used to beautify the Temple. Former oppressors will humbly recognize the City as "the Zion of the Holy One of Israel." Jerusalem, so long desolated and deserted, will be the very mistress of the nations, and will learn by a new experience that the Lord is the "Saviour," the "Redeemer," the "Mighty One of Jacob" (vs. 10–16).

The prosperity of the city is pictured as though its brass were turning to gold, its iron to silver, its wood to brass, its stones to iron. Righteous rulers will secure such peace and protection that the walls of the city will be called "Salvation" and its gates "Praise." Its real splendor will not depend on sun or moon, but the Presence of God will be its unfailing light. To a righteous people, greatly enlarged in number, the land will be given as an everlasting heritage. All this blessedness will be the gift of the divine Redeemer who declares,

I the Lord will hasten it in its time (vs. 17–22).

When would this time come? When would the prediction be fulfilled? Undoubtedly the prophet had in mind the Return from Babylon and the Restoration of the City. Yet he employs figures of far wider application. The "glory of the Lord" which was to arise on the nations would be none other than that which was embodied in the divine Saviour, the "Light of the world." As for the City, it was surely a symbol of the New Jerusalem, the Bride of the Lamb, the Church of Christ, which John saw and described in terms borrowed from this prophecy:

And the city had no need of the sun, neither of the moon, to shine in it: for the glory of God did lighten it, and the Lamb is the light thereof. And the nations of them which are saved shall walk in the light of it: and the kings of the earth do bring their glory and honour into it. And the gates of it shall not be shut at all by day: for there shall be no night there (Rev. 21:23–25).

As to the ultimate fulfillment of the prophecy which immediately follows (Ch. 61:1–3) we have the assurance of the Saviour Himself. The words carry us forward to the scene in the synagogue at Nazareth, and we hear our Lord reading the lesson from "the prophet Isaiah":

The Spirit of the Lord is upon me, because he hath anointed me to preach glad tidings to the poor; he hath sent me to heal the brokenhearted, to preach deliverance to the captives, and recovering of sight to the blind, to set at liberty them that are bruised, to preach the acceptable year of the Lord (Luke 4:18, 19).

Then Jesus added His arresting claim: "This day is this scripture fulfilled in your ears." The ancient prophecy was thus an outline and picture of the gracious ministry of Christ and of the glorious salvation which He provides.

This was the Saviour's definite interpretation of the prediction; but the words, when first spoken, applied to the deliverance of the Jews from Babylon and to the Restoration of Jerusalem. The prophet, or the "Servant of the Lord," was anointed by the Spirit to bring the glad tidings of "liberty to the captives," "to comfort all who mourn," "to give them beauty for ashes," "the garment of praise for the spirit of heaviness," that the Lord "might be glorified" (Ch. 61:1–3).

The previous chapter emphasized the material prosperity of the restored City; here, in the verses which follow, chief stress is laid on its spiritual renewal and on its priestly service. Physical splendor, indeed, is promised: ancient ruins are to be built up, devastated cities are to be repaired; political supremacy is promised, foreigners are to be their shepherds and plowmen; yet the chief glory of the people is to be that they are to carry out the original mission of Israel, and are to represent to the nations of the world the true and living God.

> You shall be called the priests of the Lord, men shall speak of you as the ministers of our God.

When true to this high destiny, they will receive from the nations respectful homage, and will be recognized in their true character as the people whom "the Lord has blessed" (vs. 4–9).

This inspiring message closes with a song of praise. It is the voice of the divine Servant who identifies Himself with the redeemed people. Salvation has been assured, and the nation is to be vindicated before the world:

> I will greatly rejoice in the Lord,
> my soul shall exult in my God;

for he hath clothed me with the garments
of salvation. . . .
The Lord God will cause righteousness
and praise
to spring forth before all the nations (vs. 10, 11).

The redemption and vindication of Zion have come,
however, only in the sense that they exist in the purpose and promise of God; but they are soon to be
manifest. The Intercessor will not be silent until they
appear. There is no uncertainty in the mind of the
Speaker. He affirms that the nations would be witnesses of the great event. A new name would be given
to the City corresponding to her glorious character.

You shall no more be termed Forsaken,
and your land shall no more be termed Desolate;
but you shall be called Hephzi-bah (i.e., "My delight is in her")
and your land Beulah (i.e., "Married");
for the Lord delights in you,
and your land shall be married.

The land would be called "Beulah" because the people would be "united" with their land. All would be
brought to pass because of the "delight" of the Lord
in Zion (Ch. 62:1–5).

The prophets stand like watchmen on the walls
to intercede for Jerusalem, and to remind the Lord
of His promises. The Lord replies. He has sworn by
His right hand that the enemy shall no longer consume
the harvests, but the produce of the land shall be en-

joyed by the people and presented as offerings in the courts of the Lord (vs. 6–9).

The Messenger now gives a summons to prepare the way before the returning exiles, for whom the nations are to serve as an escort. The deliverance would be due to the presence of a Redeemer:

> Say to the daughter of Zion,
>> Behold, your salvation comes;
> behold, his reward is with him,
>> and his recompense before him.

The nation would be known as "The holy people, the Redeemed of the Lord," and the city so long deserted would be called "Sought out, a city not forsaken." Men would resort to her to behold her glory and to promote her welfare (vs. 10–12).

The deliverance of Zion involves the destruction of her enemies. This is set forth in a dramatic dialogue. The Lord replies to the questions of the prophet. He describes Himself as a warrior returning in triumph. Alone and unaided, He has overcome all the enemies who would have retarded Israel's return.

The prophet: Who is this that comes from Edom
in crimson garments from Bozrah,
he that is glorious in his apparel,
marching in the greatness of his
strength?

Jehovah: It is I, announcing vindication,
mighty to save.

The prophet: Why is thy apparel red,
and thy garments like his that
treads in the wine press?

Jehovah: I have trodden the wine press alone,
and from the peoples no one was with
me. . . .
I trod down the peoples in my anger,
I made them drunk in my wrath,
and I poured out their life-blood
on the earth.

This is highly figurative, almost forbidding language:
but the mighty "Warrior," it must be remembered, is
also the God of love and mercy, acting only in judgment for the deliverance of His people. "Edom" is
mentioned as a type of the cruel and barbarous enemies of Israel. The "wine press" is an accepted symbol of the carnage of battle. To be "drunk" is an expression of the stupefying effect of a great catastrophe.
The main point in the poem is the fact that the "Warrior" is "alone." His solitary figure, unsupported by
horses and chariots, is to impress the truth that the deliverance of His people depends wholly on the grace
and power of the Lord.

The fulfillment of the prophecy was found in the
redemption and deliverance of Israel. By remote anal-
ogy some of its phrases are applied to the Passion of
our Saviour. The complete picture is reproduced by
the Apostle John, to present in lurid outline the final
triumph of Christ. He is to appear "clothed with a
vesture dipped in blood. . . . And he treadeth the
wine press of the fierceness and wrath of Almighty
God. And he hath on his vesture and on his thigh a
name written KING OF KINGS, AND LORD OF
LORDS" (Ch. 63:1; Rev. 19:11–16).

The dramatic dialogue, which has predicted the victory of the Redeemer, is followed by a psalm of praise. This recounts the past mercies of the Lord, and forms the basis of a prayer for deliverance out of present distress (Ch. 63:7 to 64:12).

> I will mention the loving kindnesses of the
>   Lord, . . .
>   the great goodness toward the house of Israel
>   (Ch. 63:7).

Two examples are given of the Lord's "steadfast love." The first is that of the rescue from Egypt, the second is the guidance and protection of his people on the journey to Canaan. He so trusted in their loyalty that "he became their Saviour." He so sympathized with their miseries that

> In all their affliction he was afflicted,
>   and the angel of his presence saved them.

When the people "rebelled" it was necessary for the Lord to chasten them and "to be their enemy." Then distress evoked penitence; and they "remembered" the days of old. They recalled the mercies of the Lord who had opened the sea before them, and "led them through the depths" as a horse might pass through a grassy plain. They entered the Land of Promise as "cattle" might descend from hills into the rich pasturage of green valleys. Thus "the Spirit of the Lord gave them rest" (Ch. 63:7–14).

For exactly such a deliverance, the prophet now pleads—for an exodus, not from Egypt, but from Babylon; not through the wilderness of Sinai, but on the long journey from the valley of the Euphrates to the hills of Judea.

He appeals to the Lord to "look down from heaven and see" how greatly the people need His help and compassion. The plea is based on the relation which the Lord sustains to Israel: "For thou art our Father." Even though Abraham and Jacob might not acknowledge their descendants:

> Thou, O Lord, art our Father,
>> our Redeemer from of old is thy name.

This term, "Father," so rare in the Old Testament, is for New Testament believers the most familiar word of address to God. The Creator and "Father" of Israel as a nation has come to be known as the Father of each individual who experiences a new birth through faith in Jesus Christ.

The plea is further pressed by the prophet on the ground of the present deplorable state of Israel. The people are disobedient, and their hearts are hardened and they are forgetful of God. For a short time they possessed their "sanctuary," which now their "adversaries" have "trodden down." They have become as a people over whom the Lord has "never ruled," like those who are not called by His "name" (vs. 15–19).

The pitiful statement of need is followed by an anguished cry to the Lord to intervene in behalf of His people against their enemies:

> O that thou wouldst rend the
>> heavens and come down,
> that the mountains might quake
>> at thy presence.

This would be only in accordance with the action of God in the past. He has ever delivered those who turned to Him and trusted Him and worked righteousness.

> From of old no one has heard
>> or perceived by the ear,
> no eye has seen a God besides thee,
>> who works for those who wait for him (Ch. 64:1–4).

These very words are quoted by Paul to enforce the truth that God has provided a gracious way of salvation through faith in Christ:

> Eye hath not seen, nor ear heard, neither have
> entered into the heart of man, the things which God
> hath prepared for them that love him (I Cor. 2:9).

The memory of God's mercy prompts a new confession of sin. In this confession the prophet again identifies himself with the people. If God had been displeased, it was because of their sin:

> Behold, thou wast angry, and we sinned;
>> in our sins we have been a long time,
>> and shall we be saved?

The question expresses the profoundest consciousness of guilt. Thus the prophet continues:

> We have all become like one who is unclean,
>> and all our righteous deeds are
>> like a polluted garment.

We all fade like a leaf,
> and our iniquities, like the wind,
>> take us away.
There is no one that calls upon thy name,
> that bestirs himself to take hold of thee;
for thou hast hid thy face from us,
> and hast delivered us into the
>> hand of our iniquities (vs. 5b–7).

The prayer concludes with a humble appeal for pardon and deliverance. Again the appeal is based on the fact that God is their "Father" and has brought the nation into being; He also is the "Potter," by whom the clay has been molded. Surely God will not abandon the work of His own hands.

Once again the ground for this final appeal is the pitiful condition of the holy city: "Zion is a wilderness," the Temple "burned with fire," and its "goodly buildings laid waste." Can God possibly restrain His compassion and not be moved by pity (vs. 8–12)?

By the long prayer of the prophet (Ch. 63:7–64:12) the followers of Christ may be reminded of their Master's instructions, and even may find in these earnest appeals the familiar petitions of the *"Lord's Prayer."* He taught His disciples to use the term *"Our Father"* in the largest truest sense (Ch. 63:16; 64:8). *"In heaven"* was the Father's abode (Ch. 63:15; 64:1). His *"Name"* was to be *"hallowed"* (so, Ch. 63:19; 64:7). The followers of Christ were to pray: "Thy kingdom come," and for the perfecting of that kingdom the prophet was to labor and to hope (Chs. 58–66). The *"will"* of *God* was to *"be done"* (Ch. 2:2–5;

65:17). Christians were to pray for "daily bread," to be supplied, as the Lord provided manna in the wilderness, sufficient for the need of each day. *"Forgive us our debts,"* or "trespasses," or "sins," is the very burden of this historic prayer (Ch. 64). *"Lead us not into temptation but deliver us from evil"* expresses the humility and need of divine help which is the spirit and substance of this prophetic supplication (Chs. 63:7–64:12).

To the prayer of the prophet the words of the Lord (Ch. 65) are a pertinent reply: He has ever been eager to receive and to bless those who are penitent and turn to Him; but Israel had been unwilling to come:

> I was ready to be sought by those
> who did not ask for me;
> I was ready to be found by those
> who did not seek me.
> I said Here am I, here am I,
> to the nation that did not call on my name.
> I spread out my hands all the day
> to a rebellious people.

That was the tragedy. Israel had stubbornly refused to repent, and had chosen to practice the most abominable forms of idolatry. They "sacrificed in gardens," as the heathen did; they "burned incense on bricks," or "housetops;" they "sat among graves" to receive oracles from the dead; they ate swine's flesh and drank "the broth of abominable things" which were supposed to possess magical properties; worst of all, their knowledge of unclean secrets gave them an impression that they were superior to other people, and to say:

> Keep to yourself. Do not come near me,
> for I am holier than thou."

The Lord declares His determination to visit and to destroy these apostates (Ch. 65:1-7).

Yet the nation is not to perish. For the sake of the "righteous Remnant" Israel will be saved. As a cluster may be preserved because of a few good grapes, so for the sake of His true "servants," God would spare His people, and "bring forth descendants from Jacob," and from Judah "inheritors" of the land (vs. 8-10).

On the other hand, those who forsake the Lord are "destined for the sword" and "shall bow down to the slaughter." Their fate is contrasted with that of the true "servants." The latter "shall eat," but these shall be hungry; the "servants shall drink," but these shall be thirsty; the one "shall sing for gladness of heart," the other "cry out for pain." Instead of leaving their name as a curse, the servants of God shall glorify His name as a God of righteousness and truth (vs. 11-16).

To picture the blessedness of Israel, redeemed and restored to her own land, the prophet employs a figure of speech so expressive as to be used twice in the New Testament to describe the future "restitution of all things," namely, *"I create new heavens and a new earth"* (v. 17; II Pt. 3:13; Rev. 21:1). Jerusalem, the central city, will be a scene of rejoicing, in which "weeping and the cry of distress no more shall be heard." The span of human life will be lengthened.

Men will possess houses and vineyards and enjoy them. The people will live in such fellowship with God as the prophet describes in the familiar words:

> Before they call I will answer,
>> while they are yet speaking I will hear.

In such an era of idyllic peace even the nature of the lower animals will be transformed:

> They shall not hurt, nor destroy
>> in all my holy mountain,
>>> saith the Lord (vs. 17–25).

The close of this inspired prophecy (Ch. 66) is much like its beginning (Ch. 1:1–2:4). It contains a warning against formalism in religion, a prediction of the punishment of the wicked, and of the glorious reward of the righteous.

The rebuilding of the Temple may tempt the people to feel that religion consists in erecting a structure, and in establishing a ritual; whereas true religion consists in a right relation of the soul to God. He teaches men to reverence the place of worship and to provide for its orderly service. These may aid religion but are not to be its substitutes. The Creator of the universe does not need a dwelling place made by the hands of man; He loves to abide in the hearts which are open to him in submission and trust.

Thus says the Lord:

> Heaven is my throne
>> and the earth is my footstool;
> what is the house which you would
>> build for me,

and what is the place of my rest?
All these things my hand has made
    and so all these things are mine,
        says the Lord.
But this is the man to whom I will look,
    he that is humble and
        contrite in spirit,
    and that trembles at my word (Ch. 66:1, 2).

In this view of the true nature of God and His worship
the prophet even anticipates the marvelous revelation of Christ when he declared: "God is a Spirit, and
they that worship him must worship him in spirit and
in truth" (John 4:24). He whose religion consists in
mere forms and ceremonies is, in the eyes of the Lord,
no better than an idolator. For such as are unwilling
to hear the Lord and to obey Him, severe "affliction"
is promised (vs. 3, 4).

Then, too, there are those who "hate" the righteous and "cast them out" and scoff at their religion;
surely they will be silenced and "put to shame" (v. 5).

Their mockery is answered. The prophet seems
to hear a voice in the Temple as of One preparing
vengeance:

Hark, an uproar from the city!
    A voice from the temple!
The voice of the Lord,
    rendering recompense to his enemies! (v. 6).

With this rebuke of His "enemies" and the blessing of His "servants," the remainder of the chapter is
occupied. The restoration of Israel is to be speedy; the
population of Jerusalem is to be marvelously in-

creased. Zion is compared with a woman; regenerate Israel is her child. The normal process of birth and growth are contrasted with the astonishing development of the redeemed people. It is as though a "land" should be "born in one day," and "a nation brought forth in one moment." The Lord will cause the children to rejoice and find satisfaction in their flourishing city:

> As one whom his mother comforts,
>   so I will comfort you;
> you shall be comforted in Jerusalem. . . .
>   And it shall be known that the hand
> of the Lord is with his servants,
>   and his indignation is against
>   his enemies (vs. 7–14).

These "enemies" include all who are opposed to God, even the apostates in Israel, but they designate in particular those who practice abominable idolatries. These "shall come to an end together, says the Lord."

> For behold, the Lord will come in fire,
>   and his chariots like the whirlwind,
> to render his anger in fury,
>   and his rebuke with flames of fire. . . .
> And those slain by the Lord shall be many (vs. 15–
>   17).

To these "slain" reference may be made in the last verse of the chapter, in which the prophet speaks in such appalling terms of the "dead bodies of men who had rebelled" against the Lord. They should be "an abhorring to all flesh."

Such are the last words of the chapter; but such is not the closing message of this prophecy. Its real message is that of deliverance and mercy. One must not disregard those last words of solemn warning; it was thus that the two previous sections of the prophecy ended: "There is no peace, saith the Lord, to the wicked" (Ch. 48:22; 57:21). Yet the substance of those sections, as of this chapter, is the restoration of Jerusalem and the splendor of God's perfected kingdom.

"I am coming to gather all nations and tongues, and they shall come and shall see my glory," is the promise. This prophecy of Jerusalem restored and made glorious will find its ultimate fulfillment in the perfected kingdom of our Lord. The last chapter of Isaiah points forward to the closing chapter of the New Testament (Rev. Chs. 19–22). There, when all enemies have been subdued, in "a new heaven and a new earth," the "holy city," the Church, the "Bride" of Christ, stands forth as the center of all worship, the source of all light. "The nations of them which are saved shall walk in the light of it; and the kings of the earth do bring their glory and honor into it. . . . The throne of God and of the Lamb shall be in it; and his servants shall serve him: . . . and his name shall be in their foreheads. And they shall reign for ever and ever."